# "Isolated Incidents"

## Reflections of a Correctional Officer

By

### Kevin L. Thomas

ISBN: 0-75961-390-7

This book is printed on acid free paper.

1stBooks – rev. 04/18/01

# Dedication

The writing here is dedicated to all correctional employees, past, present and future. Especially to those I worked with at Stateville Correctional Center who made my tenure a pleasant and enlightening one. Individual kudos goes out to the following: Captain Daniels (Deceased), Lieutenant Thomas, Lieutenant Mitchell, Superintendent V. C Russell, and Sergeant Bugos. There are so many officers; I would have to write another book to mention them all.

Last but not least, to all the employees who lost their lives due to no mistake of their own, except to be in the wrong place at the wrong time. Especially to those who lost their lives due to the mismanagement and incompetence of higher-ups. This book was a long time coming and I would definitely be amiss if I failed to mention Samantha, of whom was a definite and driving force periodically reminding the author of the importance of the completion of Isolated Incidents. A special thank you goes to Coco, helping the author during the intial stages.

# Table of Contents

# Preface

The completion of this book is not only imperative to the author's sanity, it is culmination of an twelve year roller coaster ride; of which this book will be the final closing. Once completed, maybe the author's family and close friends can return to some sense of normality, in respect to our individual relationships.

In and out of depression at many different levels, this writing represents a cure all, with added emphasis being put on the clarification for the reader in regards to the roller coaster previously mentioned.

Taking a ride along these ominous tracks is not a guarantee of "complete understanding" of the sights and sounds of the prison, or the myriad of feelings experienced by the author while employed at Stateville Correctional Center. I will do my best to put you "in my shoes" as they say.

In view of the fact that people visualize and feel emotion at many different levels, the author can't of course, guarantee the reader will agree in part or in whole to the words printed here. What the writer can guarantee, is that after reading cover to cover, the book in your hands, you do not feel empathy for ALL correctional officers, you need to try it for yourself. I am relatively sure my experiences were, are, and always will be, shared by every correctional officer to some extent and some more then others.

I will, as they say, be on the proverbial soapbox a good portion of the time, but that is only because the fuel of disgust is so strong for the correctional system in general, it drives the words from my thoughts not unlike a locomotive propels a train down the tracks. I honestly don't want to believe that the powers that be, orchestrate the purposeful, continued stagnation of corrections, but after eight years observing the continual cycle of incompetence, I have little else to go by.

So this is my farewell note, as lengthy as it might be. To the individuals that pretend to be running something, (and you know who you are) when in fact you watch as criminals become better criminals and whine about overcrowding. The majority of management this former correctional officer observed during their respective tenures, used words like "overcrowding" and phrases like "lengthy sentences" and "isolated incident", as swords of defense, when confronted by the slightest criticism. Some went as far as to straight up lie to the press on many different occasions.

What I observed were management wanna-bees that liked the status quo, and didn't have the gonads to facilitate serious changes in the system. One quick note in defense of some management, and most of those being middle management; is that some really wanted changes and were disgusted themselves, but when you have to feed your family, some things take precedence over others. I also understand some of the "lack of interest" I received from them when asking for assistance in reference to any obvious management slip-ups.

Bucking the system at lower levels was a quick recipe for alienation at least, and maybe even structured termination. Yes, I will attempt to give solutions as well as criticism, so that this writing doesn't weigh itself to heavily on the reader. It will be up to you to decide what your final verdict is, and maybe as a voter you can do your part to help implement changes that are badly needed. Demand to know what goes on behind the walls, don't assume. Demand that the numbers are posted, and report cards issued about each and every facility on an annual basis. Detailing expenditures, recidivism rates, murders, attacks on staff, and the like. Demand exact plans for incarceration of long-term felons and short-term felons.

Obviously this would seem a given, but in today's correctional system or at least a few years ago, convicts with one year or even less, are housed with lifer's. The same programs are offered to the lifer as to the felon doing eight months. There is something fundamentally wrong with this picture! The structure of rehabilitation and detention must be totally re-mapped, from the start to the finish. As complicated, as it will be, it must begin. My only hope is that one-day, the correctional system will be a systematic progression of change for those being reintegrated into society after they have paid their dues, and a progressive personal change for the unfortunate that must spend any extensive time behind bars. This writer also realizes that our system is not infallible, and at the same time also understands, change is a perpetual and needed ingredient in all microcosms of society. My hope is that with this writing, some with the power to do so, will take notice and begin the long needed transformation. The characters names have been altered to avoid controversy..........Kevin L. Thomas

## "Reality What a Concept"

Stateville Correctional Center is a world of itself. A little city behind aging walls of stone, it houses residents of the most despicable kind. Unwritten rules that where to complex to understand, along with "hidden agendas" that made the job as correctional officer even more dangerous then was initially anticipated. Most of which where associated directly with the plethora of problems created by the past, and at that time, current administrations.

As I went into roll call on that afternoon, I didn't realize that the officers of Unit B-East would have to deal so directly with the neglect and mismanagement that for so long had went overlooked and ignored.

Something seemed erroneous the minute we walked into the unit to start the 3-11 shift. Convicts were sticking their heads outside the bars of each gallery, and looking down the flag*. Even an officer of limited experience would be able to determine quickly that something was wrong. The cell house grapevine was also active, as we observed several groups congregating and the gangs seemed to be pairing their members up more then usual.

I just happened to be the acting sergeant on this particular shift, due to the regular sergeant being scheduled off. There where two officers that were senior to me, but they requested to go to the catwalk*. That's probably what I should have done considering the situation as it was, but I wanted more experience running the unit, so I accepted the job even though I did of course have my reservations.

B-East at the time had over four hundred inmates, and in comparison only seven officers, which included the sergeant. So I gave out the assignments and instructed the officers to be especially careful, since the word of the day was definitely caution. The catwalk officers were also instructed to be more diligent then usual and keep a careful watch on the gallery

1

officers. I did have the utmost confidence in the two officers assigned to the catwalk, since I had witnessed them fire warning shots in the past. They also had the pro-officer attitude which didn't hurt anything either.

The average Joe might think that a prison cell house of this caliber would be totally secured at the beginning of each shift. But at the 'Ville however, some rules applied and some didn't. Officers could write reports until they were blue in the face and nothing would be done. I can attest to that fact, because on too many occasions to count I tried to write the proper reports and give them to the proper brass.

So every day upon walking into the unit, the 3-11 officers first job was to secure the unit for the afternoon count. Some of the captains and lieutenants had what I would refer to as "deliberate indifference" when it came to reports that were derogatory in nature. This was partially due to their need for income and the need to feed their respective families.

So if the sergeant of the unit gave a shit, he would secure the bottom gallery himself to help facilitate the lockup. Seeing how there were only three gallery officers for the entire unit, the way I saw it, working as a team was of the utmost importance. Surprisingly enough, this particular lock up went rather smoothly and the officers completed their paperwork, passed out the mail, and then, if there was time, the officers were relieved for chow.

This also left the unit in a precarious position because more then likely the count would check, and the same inmates that were secured only an hour or so before would be let out. I'm not talking about a few of the inmates; I'm speaking of the entire unit. Those were the mind-boggling rules; let the entire unit out upon the count checking.

There were no temporary personnel to assist in this process when the officers were out of the unit. The sergeant was just expected to get the officers to chow and release the inmates immediately upon the count checking. So whomever was in the unit, would be expected to let the inmates out, regardless of whether or not one gallery officer was in the unit or the gracious compliment of three. Fortunately for the unit on this day, the officers did complete their respective tasks and get to chow and back before the count had checked.

The usual procedure was to let the entire unit out of their cells and allow them to go to the many evening programs, assignments or classes. There was also the evening meal to deal with, and later during my tenure the administration would add night visits to the itinerary. Forgive me; I forgot about gym, night yard and law library, so in a nutshell, even though we are talking of a maximum-security facility here, movement was such, that different lines* were criss-crossing each other on a continual haphazard basis.

It was literally impossible to adequately monitor movement. This officer truly believed that the best that could be hoped for, was that the roof wouldn't blow off the joint in the mean time, and by 9:30pm the inmates would somehow be safely back in their cells for the evening count. On this night however, the somewhat organized "clusterfuck" would end in an attempted murder.

So, while the institution was running wild, we had the unsavory task of babysitting four hundred plus, murderers, rapists, armed robbers, burglars and other assorted derelicts. Of course there was always the chance the different units would be taken over, but for some reason, this was rarely the case. Maybe it was because the inmates had so many privileges, that rocking the boat made no sense at all, even with their jailhouse rationale.

The inmates did their usual coming and going, and the officers did their usual praying. Psalm 23 came to mind several times during my career at Stateville.

At the 'Ville, all hell would break loose when you least expected it, and usually over something as inconsequential as cigarettes or cutting through a gangs line. My job more resembled that of a traffic cop as opposed to the security assignment to which I had been hired.

For the most part everything went as usual until we started securing the unit at 9:00pm. This was the normal practice, and the inmates for the most part were accustomed to this procedure. Start securing the inmates approximetly a half hour before count procedures went into effect and attempt to be counting same by 9:30pm.

The officers started to secure the upper galleries, while I proceeded down two gallery to secure there and begin clearing the flag. This was also a good vantage point to observe the officers on the upper galleries. I could take a few steps backward toward the wall underneath the catwalk and pretty much see all comings and goings on the upper tiers.

The unit was designed like a high rise with one gallery directly on top of one another.

I glanced at the catwalk, (which was postioned directly across from the galleries) and they appeared to be on their job so I felt a little better, even though the catwalk officers were equiped only with 4 rounds of #00 buckshot each. I had on several occasions requested an increase in the ammunition in case of a major disturbance, but as usual I received the normal earfull of bureaucratic bullshit. As I reflect back, and maybe it was because it might piss off the "inmates of power" and some bargaining ability might have been lost by the administration. We'll discuss more on that a bit later.

The inmates would play every kind of game imaginable to slow down the lockups, "I just need to get some quick smokes" or "I just need to talk to my chief for one second" and many other excuses designed to hinder the progress. Even though the majority of the cell doors in the unit could be kicked open with minimal effort, and some while they were double locked, it was still the final lockup for the night and the inmates enjoyed testing the officers regardless. This was a usual game for them, dipping and dodging as long as possible, the phrase "fuck the police" was not uncommon to hear while walking down a gallery.

As I explained before, there were five galleries, each of which had fifty-eight cells. Most of the cells were two man cells, which made it even more difficult for securing purposes. A few of the cells actually did work properly, but there were no gates at the ends of the galleries. The bars on the outside of the galleries, were missing or damaged to the point that the inmates climbed up and down like spiders on a web. Up and down, up and down, with no fear whatsoever.

On the humorous side, they were pretty good at it too. I could be securing on the bottom gallery, head to the top gallery to assist an officer, and see an inmate walking around that I had just secured only minutes before! The funny thing was he had never used the stairs. Officers were written up on many occasions for miss-counts. Many receaving suspensions and losing needed pay. Obviously directly related to the aforementioned inadequacies.

Again, the powers that be, would have a hard time understanding the correlation between miss-counts and inoperable doors. An inmate might be in one cell one minute and in a completely different cell the next. With both doors appearing totally secured to the naked eye. So as a new officer it was really a bitch, and you had better learn faces really quick. I was really lucky during my time in population, as I did't receive many write-ups for miss-counts. This was of course all luck and I acknowledge that fact.

Well anyway, I began walking down the flag and everything seemed ordinary (if there was such a thing). The inmates were locking up slowly, but not to the point of scrupulous concearn. We did have a lieutenant assigned to the unit and he did help secure on many occasions. Unlike many other white shirts that prefered running the unit from their offices via a radio. Lieutenant Tomms was different, and soon I would see why.

Out of my peripheral vision, I saw, what appeared to be two inmates boxing. At first glance I dismissed this as convict games, but when I saw a pair of glasses go flying, I realized this was more serious then I first thought. I did have about half the inmates on two gallery secured but of course that really didn't mean a damn thing.

I immediately got on the radio (which by the way was the only piece of equipment an officer was issued) and told the catwalk there was a 10-10* in progress on the flag by the fire escape. As I ran over to attempt to break up the fight and hope that I received backup, I noticed about eight to ten Latin Kings* climbing down the outside of the galleries to the flag. It appeared they were coming to assist one of their brothers* beat the shit out of another inmate.

The inmates scaling down the galleries had weapons in hand. Things began to happen very quickly at this point, but in slow motion at the same time. A kind of sureal athmosphere actually. As the inmates hit the flag, I noticed that their weapons consisted of broomsticks of different lengths and shanks*. Only a couple of minutes had actually passed, but the sureal environment made it seem like hours, while I tried to keep the inmates from each other and waiting for the backup to arrive.

Trying to keep the inmates apart was a task in itself, and the catwalk did manage to fire two warning shots into the ceiling, attempting to slow or stop the melee. This neither stopped or slowed down the events. Two thoughts came to mind at this point; One, the inmate I was trying to protect must not have been in a gang because no other inmates were coming to his aid, and two, with this many inmates on the flag facing me, why hadn't I been seriously hurt already. Fortunately for me, the inmate being attacked was not in a gang. If he had been, I definetly would have had a much more serious situatiuon on my hands. This would have been gang against gang.

The Kings could have seriously hurt me at any given time. All I sustained was a welt from a broomstick I blocked with my forearm. A very long three to four minutes had elapsed, when I observed Lieutenant Tomms running towards me with C.S* gas in both hands. One of the canisters was the fogger type, designed to spray a large area. The other was intended as a streamer for more accurate shots. A lot was happening with more then a dozen people involved in kind of a violent dance, and as such, Lieutenant Tomms was spraying everything moving, including this officer. The catwalk did not fire anymore shots, and I would learn later that was because their view was obstructed by the fire escape we were under, that stretched from the floor to the ceiling.

One of the Latin Kings did manage to get around us and stab the inmate in the neck and in the process, sprayed a pretty grotesque design on my uniform shirt. Only one officer assigned to the unit came to assist us during the entire incident. The two that didn't respond, claimed they had no idea what was going on. Even though shots fired inside the building echo so loud, you would swear a volcano had erupted.

We were somehow holding our own, other than the stabing, when I looked up and saw Major Shoegig and a bunch of whiteshirts coming towards us. The had been advised of the situation via main control and had come from out side the unit in the tunnels somewhere.

When the inmates realized the calvary had arrived, they gave up their attempt at killing the inmate, and started running back to their respective cells. The same way they arrived, up the galleries courtesy of the missing and broken bars on the front of the galleries.

I would find out later Lieutenant Tomms had sprayed everyone concerned for more then just to take some control. When a person is gassed, his face becomes beet red with irritation and their eyes tear. This doesn't go away in a short period of time. So after we calmed things down, and made sure the unit was as secure as possible, we went back onto the galleries and we were able to pick out most of the inmates involved just by looking at their faces!

Some of the inmates did manage to clean up their act prior to our walking about a half dozen to segregation. I also would find out the next day that the inmate that was attacked, was under the umbrella* of the Gangster Disciples*. They hadn't jumped in though, because they thought we were doing ok protecting the inmate and they were actually getting a kick out of watching us do just that. The inmate being attacked wasn't an actual G.D., but was only under their unbrella and as such wasn't as valued I guess.

The unit went on lockdown* due to the events of the evening. Everyone involved filled out the proper paperwork and the shift ended. The funny thing, I thought at the time, was that an old man with a cane and one officer held off more then ten attackers with weapons until help arrived. I enjoy thinking about it like that anyhow.

The following day I found out that the Lating Kings were attempting to charge the old man rent for his cell, of which they claimed as their own. This is a usual event in the life of inmates.

Obviously the old guy wouldn't go for it and that started the ball rolling. The old man was transferred to another institution later that evening. About three months had passed when I heard that he had died. I would like to think it wasn't from complications caused by the stab to his neck and he died of natural causes, but I know different. I didn't realize it at the time, but since I had attempted to help the old man I had earned the respect of many of the cellhouse inmates. Little did I know at the time, but an officer helping an inmate in a life or death situation is an immediate way to receive needed respect. I also learned that if the Lating Kings didn't respect me or my correctional style in the first place, the whole evening would have ended much differently.

I learned a lot from the events that occurred that evening. Some of which would help me later along my travels through the Stateville maze.

The story really didn't begin here though. So lets go to the place where stories start best, the beginning.

## "Getting on Board"

I met Alec Bender on a breezy night in June of 1988. He was a stocky individual with a short military style haircut. He had an "I don't give a rats ass" stride and demeanor that would rival most hard-core gang members. Four or five times a week he would stop in and buy his usual two packs of Marlboro cigarettes on his way to work. Alec was a correctional officer at Stateville Correctional Center, located in Northern Illinois. I on the other hand, was working my way up the corporate ladder, via the local convenient store/gas station.

Slowly, Alec and I became friends. Rather than just exchanging pleasantries, we began to talk about our families and our respective jobs. Alec was an extremely likable person once you got past the wall that seemed to totally encompass him. Always appearing with a touch of stress outlining his face, he seemed to hold this look as long as we discussed his job. If we veered off the subject of his work, those seemingly indented stress lines would slowly disappear. Once again reappearing at the slightest mention of Stateville.

I found out shortly thereafter that he had been a correctional officer for a little over eight years. He said he stayed at the job for the employment security and the income, which wasn't too shabby. Since I too had a family, I cautiously asked about Stateville Correctional Center. He told me that the position of correctional officer started at about twenty thousand a year. It also had good benefits, of which included medical, dental, and eye care for the whole family. Holidays were fair; in that you received thirteen paid holidays, twelve sick days, and three personal business days per year. As well as two weeks paid vacation after the first year. I would find out later, some of those benefits were hard to come by.

Since the corporate ladder previously mentioned was nowhere to be found, I asked for and received an application from my new friend. A week or so later, Alec dropped off a packet containing the application. On the front of the application was a cover letter that welcomed "the applicant" to the Illinois Department of Corrections hiring process. Of course like most people, I definitely had my reservations, but it sounded like it beat the hell out of my current situation.

With my family in mind, some soul searching and deliberations with my better half, I began filling out the lengthy application.

The application itself was four or five pages long and consisted of what I thought were fair questions for this kind of employment. It asked for specific information regarding the last ten years of employment, along with a complete educational background. Inquiry was also made regarding business and personal references. The application was rather extensive and seemed to cover all the bases.

After mentioning the prospect of becoming a correctional officer to family and friends, I received a few strange looks, as well as some well placed snickers. This might have had something to do with the fact that my stature at five feet, six inches tall; and one hundred and forty-five pounds, didn't fit the pre-conceived notion of a prison guard.

A few days later I ran into Alec at the station and gave him the fully completed aforementioned document and asked him to do what he could.

I had hoped to manage a store soon, and maybe even own a business of my own some day. My thoughts also were that the convenience store wasn't that bad, and I actually enjoyed a lot of the customers. As I contemplated the two scenarios, it seemed that these thoughts were more of a pipe dream then reality. I was in my late twenty's and going nowhere fast. So with a little luck and the grace of god, maybe I would actually be starting an actual career soon.

For approximately three weeks, every other day or so, I asked Alec if he had heard anything. I know this started to annoy him, but I was excited at the prospect of doing something legitimately constructive for once. I had just about started to write this so called dream job off, when to my surprise the phone rang at my home and it was the training school at Stateville Correctional Center. I was speaking with Officer Witt who was second in command to Lieutenant Galapagos.

He informed me that "the application had been accepted and processed, and barring any problems with the usual FBI check I was right on schedule and the paperwork appeared fine up to this point." He explained the next step of the hiring process would involve my physically going to Stateville and taking some written, physical and verbal tests. I was told to wear loose fitting clothing for the agility tests. I was also told to bring the following items to the interview: Birth Certificate, High School Diploma or GED, a copy of my DD214 (Military Discharge) if applicable, a copy of college transcripts, and photo ident-ification, preferably a drivers license. He also made it perfectly clear that if any of the documents mentioned were omitted, the applicant would be refused the chance to screen on that particular date. I put together the documents requested, and on the following Monday set out for the sinister grounds of Stateville Correctional Center for testing. The drive was about forty-five minutes west of my home mostly by highway.

As I arrived early on that sunny Monday morning, I observed a lengthy drive leading to the prison. The prison itself, with its concrete walls and gun towers on the corners, looked pretty intimidating if not down right ominous. So I won't lie and say I didn't consider turning around and forgetting the whole thing. (Because I did!) This integrity thing kept getting in the way though, and the prospect of going back to the convenience store with my tail between my legs didn't seem too savory. So I decide I wasn't stopping there.

I would be informed later that the prison had walls that were thirty-three feet high with fourteen wall towers, some operable and some not. This should have been my first clue, that at least some neglect had taken place in the past. Since the prison had been built over sixty years before, I dismissed that thought, and my gullibility convinced me that time was the culprit and not necessarily negligence.

The gatehouse was the first building that I would encounter. It's primary function was to screen visitors whether or not they were there for business or to visit a convict; and to shakedown* all employees and packages. The process appeared to be pretty antiquated, to say the least, and this should have been my second clue to the daily operations at Stateville. Again I failed to heed to the obvious.

The officer assigned to the gatehouse, gave me one of those stick-on "Hi I'm Kevin" name tags. I then waited with approximately twenty other people, while we all tried to look equally confident and unconcerned about the future. Actually, I was pretty freaked out about the whole thing, and therefore, I'm not sure my self-imposed mask helped at all.

The wait lasted more than thirty minutes, and I wondered why the training school staff was not more prompt. Finally we were escorted to the administration building, which housed the training school on the third floor. The mailroom and assorted managerial offices are housed there as well.

When I arrived at the training school I would finally meet Bill Witt in person. We had talked a few times, and I was curious what he was actually like. He explained to the officer hopefuls, that if they passed this phase of the hiring process they would also have to pass a urinalysis and then a blood test. Both of which would occur on different dates.

So we began our quest with some fundamental math and verbal tests. The tests were supposed to have been on the tenth grade level, but I found them to be more of the "do you have a brain type"? Even with the simplicity of the tests, more than half of the potential correctional officers failed, and I never seen or heard from them again. They were instructed that they could come back after a designated period of time and try the tests again if they felt so inclined.

The physical agility tests were interesting in that they encompassed quite a few areas and I was starting to think that maybe the Illinois Department of Corrections was for real. In view of the fact that a lot of the applicants had been weeded out, and there was a lot of the day left, it seemed as though the Department of Corrections was being very selective as far as new employees were concerned. This was just another bunch of smoke and mirrors that I would learn down the road, was all just part of the game.

Well, anyway, we started the physical tests with a simple toe touching exercise that would apparently give a suitable example of our flexibility. We were then required to do a set amount of push-ups to ascertain upper body strength.

Balance would be evaluated by completing a standard known as the circle walk. This was an interesting state of affairs of which the tested individual had to place his or her finger on a designated spot on the ground, walk around that same spot, not at anytime lifting the finger from the ground. Then, stand, and walk a ten-foot line requiring three or four steps. The whole time, both feet touching that same line. The two obvious failing points being, lifting your finger off the spot on the ground while making the continual circles or at anytime one or both of your feet not touching the line. My balance appeared to be acceptable and so I went on to the next assessment.

The next test would fall under the endurance category and involved running in place for two minutes, keeping an approximate pace of one-hundred and eighty steps per minute. All the while estimated and judged by the staff of the training school. You would then stop abruptly, and hold your breath for a designated amount of time. At first, this test appeared to be there for the amusement of the instructors, but it must have had some validity, because we lost some people here as well.

We then were treated to some Stateville cuisine in the employee chow hall. It was not that I saw a rather large cockroach on the wall that bothered me, but the fact that convicts were serving the food. It seemed logical that "inmates" might prepare "inmates food", because they would be less likely to tamper with it, but preparing and serving officers food seemed to be pushing the envelope a bit much. Well, I was hungry, the day had been busy, and besides all the other fools were eating. So I had what I would soon realize was one of their core entrees; chicken, hoping all along with the other idiots that the inmates hadn't tampered with it in any way.

After approximately an hour, we went back up to the training school for the final phase of the testing. The very last roadblock to the training academy in Springfield would be an oral interview with some of Stateville's "higher-ups". I would find out later these higher-ups were unit supervisors.

They asked several "what if?" scenario questions designed to trip up the person being interviewed. Thanks to my old buddy Alec, who told me to be especially cautious during this part, I gave my replies a lot of deep thought before I actually answered.

The tests had taken the majority of the day, and Bill Witt explained to the handful of people that had made it this far, that we would be contacted later the following week with information regarding the urinalysis and blood work.

On Friday of the following week, Bill Witt phoned and said the urinalysis would be held the following Monday, first thing in the morning, at Joliet Correctional Center. Joliet Correctional Center was just a few miles from Stateville, and appeared like an old Scottish castle. It had those "chess like" rook corners and weathered gold stone. Joliet was also a maximum-security prison, but was used mostly as a screening and distribution point for new convicts introduced into the system. The urinalysis itself only took a couple of minutes, but the wait was like two hours.

Another week or so had gone by, when I was again contacted by the training school, and advised that I had passed the urinalysis. The good news came about ten minutes before my scheduled Friday afternoon shift at the convenience store. Bill Witt advised me to report at six in the morning the following Monday. At which time, the correctional officer trainees would be taken by bus to the training academy in Springfield.

So I went to work that evening with a strange mix of accomplishment and uncertainty. That night at the convenience store was probably the best I ever had. Since optimism was now part of my life I had to share the good news with almost every customer that walked in the door. Finally the night would come to an end, and I was locking the door for the last time. I didn't realize it then, but I was about to enter the most bizarre environment I had ever experienced. One of the last customers of the night was Alec. I thanked him religiously for his help and guidance up to this point. One thing kept thundering through my head as I drove home; on Monday morning the trek to the training academy in Springfield would begin, and no one would be around to help me then.

The morning did come, and Alec offered to accompany me to the prison. The day was crystal clear and I was hoping this was an omen concerning my decisions of the past month or so.

The itinerary would be the same for the following six weeks. Arrive at Stateville early on Monday mornings, travel on a uncomfortable converted school bus for more then three and a half hours, stopping at all prisons in the upper half of the state; picking up other officer trainees, then unpack my belongings once we arrived at the academy. On Fridays, I was allowed to make the same trip in reverse and spend the weekends with my family at home. Even though my days were filled with classes, lectures and demonstrations, the Mondays came quickly, and the Fridays at a notably lackadaisical pace.

The evening before I left for my first week at the academy, my family acquired a dog. The dog was a German Shepherd/Collie mix. His name was Bear and he barked viciously. I hoped this would make my family feel more secure and give me a little more piece of mind as well. He would eventually die, about three years after my resignation from Stateville. Doing all along, what I had initially requested of him. Barking his brains out.

# "The Training Academy"

I am sure the instructors had good intentions as far as relaying information to aid us in becoming informed correctional officers. I am also relatively sure the C.O.Ts* from the minimum and medium facilities benefited greatly from what was taught.

On the other hand, the officers from the maximum joints were only going through the motions. Mostly due to the fact that the instructors were teaching from an "as it should be done angle" and the maximums were for the most part, not in this group. The C.O.Ts from the max joints were for the most part, just killing time. I would soon learn Stateville especially, was infamous for being deficient when it came to playing by the rules.

On the flip side of that coin, I did learn how to operate and clean three different weapons. Those included the Smith and Wesson #38 Model 10, as well as the Ruger Mini-14 rifle and the Remington 870 Wingmaster, All preferred weapons of many law enforcement agency's and prisons in the country. I did, to my surprise, qualify expert on the three weapons combined.

All officers were required to re-qualify yearly at their respective institutions. I would attain the expert rating every single year except the last year I was tested, when I bought a pair of glasses to help my astigmatism and near-sightedness. On that particular year, I just missed expert by a few points and attained the sharpshooter title. Then again there was always a running joke at the 'Ville. Which in part stated, "If you shoot expert, and your involved in a killing, you might have a bit more explaining to do. If of course you qualified less then expert, there would be a reasonable doubt as to your accuracy". If an expert at the time of a shooting, you might have to explain your actions with a little more detail to justify a critical shot. Obviously, less then expert would give you the "misses now and then wild card". That joke seemed in bad taste, but then again, it did have some validity.

We also had classes on Administrative Directives and Departmental Regulations; affectionately referred to as AD's and DR's. These were supposedly the heart and soul of the entire state prison system. Stateville turned these rules off and on like a water faucet, to satisfy their own particular needs. (Speaking of the water at Stateville, DON'T drink it. More on that subject a bit later.) I learned that the Stateville administrations were selective to say the least, as to when and where a particular rule applied. By word of mouth, I also would learn that the other institutions were without a doubt, less pliable when it came to the rules.

In hindsight, it seemed that my time at the academy went rather quickly and each day was filled with enough material to keep the recruits fairly busy. After dinner you had the choice of studying or getting together in the game room for the latest gossip. Of which I noticed right away, had the air of a soap opera. So I pretty much kept my distance and used the time to study the materials given.

A few recruits even ventured off campus, which was expressly forbidden. Some were caught, and some weren't. The individuals that were caught had wasted their time up to this point, because leaving the campus was grounds for immediate termination. This seemed like a fair judgment, because we were made aware of this rule clearly from the start.

We also received some rudimentary instruction on gangs. One of the few things I was able to put to use in actual situations. This subject matter with out a doubt was the best covered of all I would learn at the academy. The instructors for the most part, were very enthusiastic about what they were teaching; it's just that the max-joints were a totally different world then what the teaching appeared geared for.

Stateville especially stood out in this, as it was also an example in class. "The instructors referred to the "standard way" and the "Stateville way". The instructors had no problem conveying this fact repeatedly. They just didn't seem to elaborate much when making this statement. I could only surmise, that whatever I learned should be taken like a grain of salt, because of the obvious lack of clarification. At first I thought the instructors were just picking on Stateville because there were only two recruits out of a class of sixty-three. The final summation came to this; Stateville was not the jewel of the state as far as the Department of Corrections was concerned.

The highlight to the six weeks at the academy had to have been the dreaded fifth week. This would be when all the recruits would venture as a group, to one of the three max joints in the state, and conduct a mass shakedown*. It shouldn't have been a surprise to me when Stateville was selected as the location for this little field trip. They usually went to one of the maximum-security prisons for this little field trip.

Usually the choice for the shakedown was random and routine, and was meant to be just an experience for the new recruits. This time though, Stateville had just had an employee murdered. This would make this little jaunt, a bit more on the realistic side.

Usually this trip would involve simple shakedowns, with the officers looking for major contraband. On this trip though, the instructors even seemed keyed up, and the rookie's would be told to "take everything but their dreams" both at the academy and again when we arrived at Stateville. Meaning that we should take everything not state issued. This comment brought a couple thoughts to mind. First, why should this shakedown be any different then any other, and second, why would the inmates have belongings not issued by the state to begin with? I understood the words revenge and retribution, but what I didn't understand was the fact that either something is contraband or it isn't. To me it shouldn't make a difference if someone was killed or not. If a convict has contraband items, they should be confiscated and the proper reports written. The thought of fair play and integrity seemed to come to mind here.

We did, in fact, go to the 'Ville and conduct a shakedown. I was told the inmate had killed a commissary worker for a case of cigarettes, and some other odds and ends. What struck me odd was that the employee was killed in the early morning hours when he opened the commissary. The inmate that killed him had somehow managed to pass several gates and cameras to accomplish this act. Again this should have been a red flag, but again I failed to heed the warning. The Polish part of me had determined, that movement like this must be a common occurrence at a maximum-security prison. Considering I had no experience in such an environment, I really still don't feel I should have quit then, although a few recruits did exactly that.

The inmate was apparently attempting to pay off a debt and the killing was not sanctioned* by the gangs. The day in itself was pretty enlightening, though a touch on the frightening side. The inmates were also keyed up for obvious reasons, and the institution was very noisy. They knew with an employee death they were in for a long lockdown. The recruits still seemed to get through it all, without so much as a scratch.

One thing that disturbed me was the fact that it seemed several times during the day, I could have sworn a certain object had been removed from a cell, and then when I would pass that same cell later in the day, the object somehow magically re-appeared.

Also in the mix, was the fact that we had worked under several different lieutenants. They all seemed to have their own rules regarding contraband. Some had a no tolerance policy and seemed to go strictly by the rules, tickets and all, while others varied about which items were serious enough to even mess with. So when I passed cells that had contraband that we had already shook down, I felt hard pressed to say anything at all. I found it very easy for me to dismiss these notions to the drama of the day.

After I would finally arrive permanently at Stateville, I would realize I wasn't imagining things, and that I really didn't have a clue what was actually going on. Another red flag, and damn, I'm not even color blind; so I had no excuses.

Well in the end, the class did graduate, and we moved onto our respective assignments. I was ranked eleventh out of the class of sixty-three officers.

# "Let the Games Begin"

When I arrived for my first week of orientation, I felt at the time, I had learned a lot and that should help make the transition easier. What I found out rather abruptly was that, I might as well have forgotten everything I had just learned, and cleared my memory banks. The things I had just been taught while at the academy did not apply to Stateville, because as I was told several times in many different ways was "we do things our own way here at Stateville". This was reiterated on several occasions by the training school staff. This would also really confused me, but I attempted to initiate the learning process from the beginning once again.

The majority of the weeklong orientation consisted of question and answer periods, graciously separated by war stories from individuals of whom I wasn't sure even experienced those stories to begin with. Several individuals from the management levels, including the warden himself, gave their individual takes on how to do your job in the proper manner. The fact that I was a rookie didn't cloud the fact that the speeches sounded more rehearsed, then informative.

On the final day of orientation, we were supposed of had been given our first assignments. This I thought would be my first REAL challenge. This again, would also prove to be a false assumption on my part.

My first on the job assignment would be to go to the furniture factory, with NO inmates in sight. My assigned area would be at a desk close to the front door, with no movement in or out. This duty was in fact utilized when the institution was running a normal schedule. Since the institution was on lockdown, I basically had no function whatsoever. It seemed as though I was placed there, just to get me out of the way. So other than my lunch, I spent the entire shift, wandering around a deserted furniture factory, wondering why inmates of this caliber had access to electric grinders anyway.

When I walked into the institution for the first time, I did have my pre-conceived notions of what a convict and his environment were like. I am sure that picture is similar for most average people. I would learn very soon, and repeatedly, that the convicts ran the institution, and the administrations were mere puppets. Sure the brass walked around looking authoritative but the inmates were entirely to smug when confronted. I was at a loss to explain why things where the way they were, and why I had to acquaint myself with a whole set of unwritten rules. Everyone I spoke with concerning problems at the 'Ville, had his or her own opinion why things ran the way they did. Rumors ran rampant constantly changing to fit with current events.

The first thing that needed to be learned was survival. Yes of course, I am using the word survival in the literal sense, because maximum-security prisons are by definition very volatile. On the flip side, survival also meant many other things such as abiding by some of those unwritten rules. If you fit into the program and were liked by your peers and superiors (and I use that term very loosely), some infractions of the REAL rules might go overlooked. On the other hand, if you were an outcast and were disliked; EVERY rule applied and was strictly enforced. With the sole purpose, to have the individual fired at some point in time. The sooner the better!

Lets give you an example here. We had an officer that had been at the institution a few months become assigned to B-East. Lets call him Officer Biblethumper. Well officer Biblethumper would come to work every day with his personal copy of the King James Bible. Not a big one mind you, just the small pocket kind. I actually got along with him for the most part, but many officers felt this was no place for his attitude.

He talked in a soft unassuming voice and many of the officers were worried he wouldn't shoot if he had to, or maybe wouldn't even come to their aid of required. For some reason I didn't feel that way. Well by the time he had gotten to B-east he already had several write-ups under his belt and it looked as though they had put him in the cell house to continue with the strategy of writing him up on many occasions at different posts to purposely taint his record.

Lets talk about some REAL and UNWRITTEN rules that applied to inmates. Sometimes a certain inmate would have a lot of juice* and no I don't mean Sunkist. Some of the rules that were put into place for the benefit of the security of the institution would not apply to all the inmates all the time, in the exact same way. A prime example would be Richard Speck an infamous mass murderer who killed eight nurses back in the summer of 1966.

He more or less had free reign to journey anywhere he pleased in the institution. This was accomplished through the magical title of "institutional painter". Which according to anyone who was asked had the right to go where he needed to, because he had numerous assignments at several different locations. During my eight years at Stateville, I never once saw him officially escorted anywhere. He just went! This had been going on so long that even some Lieutenants and Captains were reluctant to challenge him.

Several other inmates were also allowed to move freely. Always hiding behind some job that apparently gave them carte blanche. Inmates that held most of those so-called "good" jobs were in the upper echelon of the different gangs. This might be a hard pill to swallow, but it was a fact in any case.

My first real assignment would be H-House* on the 3-11 shift. Which was supposed to have been the protective custody unit for inmates who feared for their lives for one reason or another. These inmates couldn't or wouldn't stay in population* for a myriad of reasons. Usually of which, was a certain gang wanted their ass, either literally or monetarily. Possibly for just disrespecting a member, or that inmate just being new to the system.

Whatever the reason, inmates were allowed to go to protective custody the minute they requested it. Some of the individuals that came to Stateville were not affiliated with a gang and therefor couldn't exist in the population units (Without paying a price anyway). There were a few inmates that seemed to survive on their own, but these were few and far between. The weird thing about protective custody as I said, was anyone could go at any time. All they need do was ask! This meant of course that the aggressor in the relationship could literally follow the prey to the protective custody unit. The aggressor would then bide his time until he was on the same wing as the prey or close enough to exact his vengeance up on him. This scenario played out on more than one occasion.

The ones that did accomplish surviving in population on their own were known as Neutrons*. I admired some of these guys, because they were straight up bucking the screwed up system they hadn't created. I, although a member of my own gang metaphorically speaking, was also a kind of neutron at the same time. I felt a strange kinship to those inmates that were trying to make it alone.

As I relayed in the opening of the book, sometimes a given inmate didn't belong to a gang, so the gangs extorted money from these individuals, by requiring "rent" for a cell that they claimed as their own. Sometimes rent consisted of holding contraband for a given length of time. So an inmate had a few choices, pay and stay, hold the contraband, go to the hospital, or request P.C. or punk city as it is referred to in the cell houses.

I think what bothered me the most, about the joint, was that the daily actions taken by security were very rarely uniform. Yet consistency was supposed to have been the building block of our job. The three golden rules, taught at Springfield mind you, were to be firm, fair and consistent. Firm and fair had variables, while the only thing consistent about the job was inconsistency.

Well back to the first day on the job. I had already seen a lot and didn't expect much to surprise me at this point, even though my entire time at Stateville would be filled with incessant surprises, each one seemingly more bizarre then the one immediately preceding it.

The sergeant for the 3-11 shift at H-house was Jim Knee. He assigned me to the Three-West control center. Upon arriving at the control center, I would be relieving a woman in her mid to late forties, who appeared ready to go home, to say the least. After she buzzed me in, I asked her to explain the control panels, my duties, and the procedures this assignment entailed. As she hurriedly exited, closing the door to the control center behind her, she said just one thing; "Someone will be up here shortly to answer all your questions". Guess she didn't understand the word camaraderie, or phrases like "common decency". One might even surmise, and go as far as to say she didn't even give a shit.

So I sat in the control room with fifty buttons I knew nothing about. Some had red lights and some had green lights. The easy ones were the lights that didn't work at all. At least with those, there would be no decisions to be made whatsoever. I did have a phone, but didn't know any extensions. What if one of the lights changed colors, what if there was a fire, what if an inmate suddenly appeared, what if? What if?

I stared out the Plexiglas windows for about fifteen minutes, when an officer arrived at my control room door. He motioned for me to let him in, but the designations on the buttons had been worn out over time. Not wanting to just push any button, we exchanged rudimentary hand singles for a minute or two until I figured out the proper button.

I guess he could read the confusion on my face, as he replied, "Don't panic" just don't do anything unless he or the sergeant or lieutenant of the unit told me to. He would be my gallery officer. The officer proceeded to count the inmates by opening a little viewing door located on each cell door. Some doors had to be kicked several times, to see or hear the response the officer required.

H-House was designed with two control centers at each end of the three floors. Every control center had charge over four wings. Each control center had a combined cell count of fifty. Even though logic would dictate that each cell in the unit only hold one inmate, (due to the protective custody status) there were still well over three hundred inmates assigned to the protective custody unit at any given time. Due to this obvious error in judgment, I found it pretty repulsive each time an inmate was physically or sexually assaulted by his cellie*.

The officer returned and told me I had a count of fifty inmates and told me to log it in the book on the desk, like everyone else had done on the other shifts. He also went on to tell me that anything that went on in my area of responsibility should be documented in the logbook as well. He said this was important for two reasons.

The first being that the logbook could be used in a court of law, and the second was if someone wanted a chronology of events during my shift, I could cover myself concerning my exact sequential actions throughout that shift. This also didn't make much sense, and he left the control center too quick to elaborate. I would find out in due time, what he actually meant was to be selective on entries. He of course couldn't portray those intentions by word, but I could tell by his demeanor that this was the point he was trying to convey. This also opened the door to many more questions. I decided then and there, that whatever I put in the logbook from here on out; would be as concise and neat as I could make it.

Since I was just sitting there doing nothing, I thought flipping through the logbook was a good idea, if just to critique how other officers had completed their job. What I found was a lot of entries that were illegible, or the officers had drawn derogatory cartoons or comments about Stateville in general. The majority of the logbook looked like a collage of graffiti on a viaduct or boxcar.

The lieutenant for the 3-11 shift at H-House was Rip Kroger. I would learn a little at a time, that he did things his own way and pushed the "Peter principle" to the limit. He wasn't even afraid to show me in person sometimes. This in itself should have been just another example of the many red flags I would fail to take heed to.

A good example of this, would have to have been the third day I spent in Unit-H. Lieutenant Kroger came to my control center and introduced himself for the first time. He gave me the usual welcoming; accompanied by little quips of what he thought were wisdom. At least I guess, he thought they were wise anyway. He also brought a logbook along with him, when I realized he wasn't really there to welcome me at all.

The logbook was used by the administration to keep track of phone calls made by inmates. This particular logbook was for the Three-East control center. I just happened to be assigned to the Three-West control center. So I logically thought maybe he was going to give examples of proper logbook entries or some such instruction. Well he opens the logbook, and the first thing I notice is that it hadn't been filled out for over a week. He went on to say since we were on lockdown, I basically had nothing to do, and maybe I could help him catch up on some things that were overdue. The word censurable seemed like a more appropriate word then overdue, but I acknowledged his need just the same.

I inquired as to how I was to ascertain who made what phone calls and when. His reply was that "the phone log wasn't that important, basically was a waste of time, and that I should just copy a few of the more recent pages. The phone calls were very similar each week anyway, he went on to say, and the fact the book would be up-to-date was always the most important part.

Needless to say, I actually saw this red flag, but I was NEW, and he was my NEW lieutenant. Even though this assignment was distasteful, I did as I was ordered, hoping the logbook was as unimportant as he had so eloquently portrayed it to be.

A few days later I asked an officer I knew the best and trusted, if this in fact was routine; to have filled in the logbook after the fact. He pretty much stated what I thought he would; "that the logbook wasn't really that important, but they were in fact required to be filled out completely for any audits that might occur, and that the lieutenant was just covering his own ass with a new officer." As time would go by, it seemed this was one of the lietuenants favorite maneuvers; using a new officer to do his dirty work. The officer also went on to say I was in fact falsifying documents, as inconsequential as those log books might have seemed to be.

What I didn't realize was there were logbooks for everything from inmate showers to cell shakedowns, and it was the lieutenant's responsibility to make sure these were completed in a timely fashion. I do realize now of course that all the logbooks were of extreme importance. Of course the proper thing to do as I reflect back, would have to have been to refuse the order and written a report concerning the whole incident. Maybe, just maybe, I would have still then made it through my probation and still had spent eight years at the institution as a correctional officer; but I doubt it very much.

This would be my first introduction to the phrase "hidden agendas". I realized then and there that determining which employees to trust was my prime concern at this juncture. I also realize that in all employment situations' determining the good employees from the bad is a usual concern. The only difference between the two scenarios was this wasn't some fast food restaurant or a business office downtown. This was a maximum-security prison, and mistakes in judgement on my part, could mean more than a just day or two off work!

On another occasion, when were also on lockdown, and during roll call, the shift captain explicitly stated, "no officer was supposed to open a cell door, unless it was first cleared by him personally". This very clearly made order seemed to be pretty cut and dry to me at the time, but the "last order" conundrum would rear it's ugly head at this point.

During this shift, Lieutenant Kroger came to my control center and told me to open a cell door so he could talk with the inmate inside. I had a serious problem comprehending the correlation between the need to open the cell door, and the need to talk with the inmate inside... We then had a short discussion about the order given at roll call, and continued the discussion at this point "concerning last order given" and whom was the "lieutenant of the unit". He then became a bit perturbed with my non-compliance and pushed the button himself, with a "kiss my ass attitude" and proceeded to go were he had intended to go in the first place.

He walked down the gallery went into the cell, and was only inside a few minutes. The door was then re-secured by lieutenant Kroger himself. I then had a couple choices, I could call the shift captain and explain the incident, I could write a report, or I could log what happened in the logbook. Or I could do a combination of the three things. I decided on the notation in the logbook only. This was a way to cover my own ass and not make waves at the same time. On this also, I realize upon reflection, I should have hooked this clown up big time!

This also brings to mind another weird phenomena. I refer to it as "convenient temporary amnesia". This phenomenon would occur when a superior (and again, I use that term loosely) would give an officer some instructions to carry out. If the slightest thing went wrong with the order while it was in progress, the whiteshirt* that gave the original order would have a real hard time recalling that he had in fact given the order in the first place. This situation happened routinely and the officer was left holding the bag. I realize there are cowards and back stabbers in all professions, but in this environment the effects could be more enduring.

If I was off my soapbox, let me get back on for a moment. What really sucks about the correctional system is that as an officer the odds are against you from Jump Street. You walk in the door and you don't know jack! If the inmates don't get you, alcoholism, drug abuse, marital conflicts or divorce most certainly will. When you accept the job you of course realize that a certain amount of stress comes with the territory.

Like a monkey on your back, clinging for dear life, you shake and roll trying to get rid of the pesky inflictions. Regardless of how hard you try, the monkey remains, at varying degrees. Some can handle the monkey and some cannot. Very few people do thirty years in the Department of Corrections. The ones that do are usually washed up mentally and left to ponder their pointless careers. Not that their intentions were pointless, but that the results attained were.

Hats off to those individuals regardless of their final mental state, because they are dynamos in my opinion. The turnover rate in corrections is in itself is amazing. If an officer doesn't end up resigning, getting fired, hurt or killed on the job, they usually transfer to a more placid setting. Some that seem to stick around a while are merely using the job as a stepping-stone to other positions in law enforcement. Usually if fired the factors regarding it encompass a wide range of attendance problems (of which the author can attest).

At first glance, you might say 'if you don't come to work, don't cry". The problem with this position is that in most cases, the attendance problems are caused by the monkey and or monkeys acquired while employed for the department itself. In my case, I admittedly came to the department with some baggage in hand, but the surroundings definitely had a major play in my decision to resign. Some of the worst-case scenarios I felt had a play were being killed or physically immobilized.

Corrections is not for everyone, and even to the point of being only suitable for a few personality types. So if you are contemplating a career in this field, you had better be damn sure this is what you want. I know from experience, you don't just walk away if you don't like it. You might leave the physical grounds of the prison, but the mental trips back to the penitentiary stay with you. Sometimes while you're awake, and sometimes while you're asleep. Either way, you revisit the prison often. My only advice on this is matter, is that you get as much information as possible, regarding corrections in general, and most notably about the specific institution you are applying to work at.

Another problem with attempting the correctional endeavor lies in the fact that correctional facilities as a whole are not even sure what their role is regarding the incarcerated. The laws and courts have I like to think, inadvertently made this a reality. This too leaves the correctional employee in a very precarious position.

Sixty or so years ago, a person was tried in a court of law, convicted, incarcerated, and that, as they say; was that. These individuals had no rights other than to eat and be housed. I am not an advocate of those procedures either, but the industry has done a complete 180-degree turn, in respect that the courts and prisons are confused, and continually without apparent malice use the terms incarceration and rehabilitation interchangeably. The convict not only has more rights than he did sixty years ago, he now has more rights than even the staff assigned to the institution. Don't get me wrong, I am not into a Neanderthal way of thinking, but there must be a happy medium somewhere.

Incarceration means just that; paying your dues to society for the crimes you committed. No more no less. This category would most certainly apply to the lifer's, or inmates with extended sentences that most likely will not walk beyond the confinement of the walls again. Rehabilitation on the other hand, means to change one's former negative habits and patterns and to, hopefully, re-integrate that individual back into society.

At the maximum level you have the hard-core criminals, or at least that's the way it should be. Most are doing serious time, such as at Stateville. At this point, the emphasis should be on incarceration. During the years 1988-1996 rehabilitation and incarceration were so confused at Stateville that the place was running wild. I can't speak of the time prior to 1988 as I wasn't there, and after my leaving in 1996. I do of course assume unpretentiously that it didn't sprout up magically as I arrived.

During my tenure, movement was definitely a major problem due to all the programs and activities. The inmates played this to the hilt and mostly because they could join whatever programs they wanted, pretty much without the thought of sentence structure. Whether it was a class on small engines, chess club or one of the many other activities, sentence didn't seem to play a major part. This afforded them the opportunity to move about the institution more or less unimpeded.

What I'm trying to convey in a nutshell, is this environment (Maximum) shouldn't have so many opportunities for the residents. Note to future administrations: remember the phrase "Direct Proportion"

Let's venture to the mediums for a moment. Here the dominating factor should be rehabilitation with added emphases put on incarceration. Mediums would be more suited to allow numerous programs, since the convicts here are more than likely going to be reintegrated back into society. Even here, inmates do get out of hand, but the ratio of time inmates spend outside their cells at programs, classes or whatever, should be proportional to their actions and sentences. Not to get off the beaten track, but this brings up another thought; commissary. At Stateville the commissary list was so long it took up several pages to list all the items available to the inmates, not unlike a small book. This too, should be proportional to the convicts sentencing, environment, as well as his actions and accomplishments.

Minimums on the other hand, should be geared primarily toward rehabilitation, with very little emphasis on security matters. This is not to say that these inmates too, are not convicted felons, but they will eventually, barring any unforeseen problems, return to society. Corrections should be a progressive road for the majority of the inmates and simply a "last stop" I am sad to say for those unfortunate few that have put themselves in this position to begin with. At the end of this book I will outline a potential itinerary to accomplish this.

When I started at Stateville in 1988, the place more resembled that of a college campus than that of a maximum security prison. The only function we actually had as officers was to keep the inmates from venturing beyond the confinement of the walls. Other than that, everything was up for grabs. The inmates used the overabundance of programs and activities to completely undermine what little security we had at the facility. It was physically impossible to adequately monitor movement. This is exactly what I am trying to convey as being the ineffectiveness of the situation.

To compound the problem, the last few administrations chose the bartering system as a means of communication with the gang higher-ups. In other words, the wardens would go into a kind of partnership with the more powerful gang chiefs. Of course they wouldn't admit that, and if they did, wouldn't refer to it in that FRANK MANNER. IE: "You give me this and I'll give you that". This of course might have relevance to a given job assignment or just a simple picnic. At first I'm sure it seemed like a good idea, because the chiefs do in fact have a serious amount of control over their respective gangs. The chiefs do understandably; have the power to exact serious inflictions upon the prison and or staff.

The very serious dilemma here lies in the fact that when the brass crossed the line between ordering and bartering, there was no turning back. A hypothetical arrangement might go like this: You (the chief) keep your people in line next week, no assaults or whatever; I (the warden) have the governor coming to look around. I (the warden) want this place running like a clock. And I (the warden) will give you a picnic on the yard the following Sunday.

NO arrangements should have ever taken place. The one thing I did learn while employed at the prison, is the prisoners' want what they have coming to them, no more and no less. That is a fair arrangement and should be consistently managed. When you start giving more than they have coming, they start to expect those extras as well. Not to mention the fact that once you go into the negotiating mode, you open up a whole new Pandora's box.

Officers never really knew at any given point where their authority started and ended, especially with high-level gang members. The inmates had this smug attitude more or less; if they didn't like a certain officer's actions, they felt that they could easily go see someone else higher up on the ladder and have the situation put in to a favorable light. They could do this, because they knew that if the administration didn't have respect for them in the first place, they would not have negotiated any deals in the first place. This in itself gave them unlimited bargaining power for the duration, at all different levels.

This created other problems as well. For example: The fact that certain inmates had more privileges than other inmates solely because of relations with the administration and or their rank in the gang hierarchy secretly pissed off many of the other more manageable inmates. Some of those inmates were not even of the troublesome type, but this injustice would piss them off to no end. As such, those usually controllable inmates only had the front line officer to dump those feelings on. So it went, day after day, an unnecessary soap opera.

The problem too, was that no one knew at any given time, which deals had been made and with whom. No one, at least on the front line employee level, ever knew where the administrations held their loyalties. The one inmate I remember most that seems to fit this to a tee was the one I would refer to as the "Arizona Kid". He either had really pissed off the administration or had entirely too much shit to talk about. In either case, like an unexpected storm, he was whisked from

Stateville and suddenly transferred to Arizona. Which seemed a bit interesting since one of our illustrious wardens had previously been employed there. This story is only conjecture on my part. You of course, are free to come to your own conclusions!

Stateville was such a place. Gross negligence and mismanagement are not too strong of terms when describing day-to-day operations. Whoops, did I say operations. The administrations were like those proverbial monkeys; …you know the ones… hear no evil, speak no evil, see no evil… yea those. Speak no evil was definitely the most important of the three. Since the last thing the state or prison officials wanted was information leaking out about the bullshit going on behind the walls! "Hear no evil" and "see no evil" were important also because they went hand in hand with "speak no evil", but as far as the brass was concerned, the main thing was shut the fuck up!

Yea, it pisses me off. A lot of good people paid unnecessarily, and for all the wrong reasons. Well I'll get of my soapbox for a while and we'll jet back to the 'Ville, although be prepared, I am sure I will get back on.

I really felt, even with what I had experienced already that it would be best if I tried to be a team player. I really tried hard to pull my own weight, since I was a Correctional Officer Trainee. This would prove to be difficult. I soon found out that officers, who worked hard, were worked hard. The officers who were non-productive or pretended to be, were given assignments requiring very little.

Because at the time I was too naïve to notice this, I was usually on the galleries dealing directly with the convicts, while the unproductive types, sat on their collective lazy asses in control centers or similar non-contact assignments. Looking back, I guess they were the intelligent ones after all. I'm the one writing this, and they more than likely are still sitting in their chairs like an unmovable gargoyle, watching the continuous procession of idealistic employees come and go. I also led myself to believe in the hope of sustaining my mental strength, that the sergeant and lieutenant had a lot of faith in me, so I continued working the galleries night after night.

From the sergeants point of view, and I do understand; with the idiots out of the way in unassuming posts, he had people on the galleries that he thought would get things done. I also tried to use this continual mental argument as another motivational tool and as such making his and my profession that much easier. The quandary here is that from the officers standpoint, burnout began to be a real part of life. I didn't know it at the time, but those monkeys on my back were already gaining ground.

While the officers in the control centers remained relatively unscathed, the gallery officers job included but not limited to, moving several lines a night, shaking down cells, moving inmates from one unit to another, making security checks, breaking up scuffles, and anything else the sergeant or lieutenant could think of.

I started to feel like the proverbial eight ball. In the line of fire on most shifts, I started to inquire as to why things went the way they did. To the officers who were in the control centers most of the time, and to the staff assigning me to the galleries on an almost daily basis, this appeared as whining. I also realized they liked to use that exact fact as another reason to put me back on the galleries. So it really didn't matter if I complained or put up with the shit. I ended up for the most part along with a few others, doing the dirty work.

I decided to stop complaining at some point, although I don't remember the exact time, because I realized the complaining used up mental energy I desperately needed. I kept trying to think of my family, the pay and benefits. These thoughts weighed heavily enough at this point to drive me on.

The unit sergeant and lieutenant eventually tried a new tactic. They took my naivete to a new level, by leading me to believe that my presence on the galleries helped the unit run smoothly. I badly wanted to believe this, and with the monkey chewing away night after night, I attempted to work hard and hold my head up.

I started to notice more and more inconsistencies in the way the unit was run, and since I was starting to learn the ins and outs of the job, I was just about to really question procedures, when a notice came in my mailbox at work. It stated that, "I had been bumped by a senior officer". I would, at the first of the month, assigned Unit B-East. Since Unit B-East was a population unit with a whole new set of problems, I thought maybe I should have kept my mouth shut.

The timing would be real good or real bad depending on your point of view. Either way, one lives and learns, I guess. The time span up to this point; had been eight months since my arrival from the training academy.

## "Out of the Pan, into the Fire"

I had just started to think of Unit-H as my home and was beginning to get comfortable with the surroundings. I was likewise beginning to learn the faces and attitudes of the different inmates, and so this new move was going to be just like leaving the academy all over again. In hindsight, it seemed that the change in venue, was just to mess up my bearings. Then again, that's just my opinion. I was though, essentially starting from scratch, and since I had this feeling several times before, I started to believe this was the over all goal, to keep one guessing and uncertain of things to come. In defense of the office boys, bump slips were continually en' route as they say.

I did learn an interesting trivia fact the first day I entered Unit B-East. B-House was the longest rectangular cell house in the world, and was documented in the Guinness Book of World Records. I never actually confirmed this little bit of infamy, but I felt it seemed to bode well with the over all scheme of things.

The sergeant and lieutenant in this unit were much more to my "first impression" liking and so maybe the move was a godsend. A "give and take" kind of thing I guess...more dangerous unit, but more competent bosses. I felt at this point, I would make the trade without reservation.

I had already witnessed several officers junior to me, as well as senior, come and go, for one reason or another. Because of this, I started to wonder if longevity was a legitimate concern. What actually was my function here, and was I a pawn to be moved as needed? Would I eventually be gone for one reason or another and was I just wasting my time? I try real hard to stay off that soapbox, but feelings rush back and overwhelm me as I try and paint an accurate portrait for you the reader.

Of course you must keep in mind, these are reflections of the past, and many changes have definitely taken place in the author's persona. These feelings are so strong about those past experiences, that sometimes my thoughts go ninety miles an hour, and I have a hard time expressing my feelings properly. Please forgive me, if I appear to ramble.

Well anyway, B-East was an H-House and a half to say the least. It didn't take very long at all for me to ascertain this fact.

The first day I walked into Unit B-East, there were inmates running everywhere. Not much different than ants on an ant farm. The smell of urine wasn't overwhelming, but it was there regardless. The cockroaches were definitely more plentiful than that of H-House, but like it or not, this was my new home. The inmates were also dressed a bit more free wheeling than those at H-House as well.

I met the acting sergeant, who either sensing the intimidation in my demeanor, or for the defense of his own ship, sent me to the catwalk. On his forehead in "make believe writing" I saw the words, "rookie alert".

I would find out at a later time that this was the usual procedure for a sergeant of a population unit; to introduce new officers to the cell house, via the catwalk. This way the new officers had a chance to observe more seasoned officers doing their jobs, and maybe they could make some mental notes before swimming with the sharks. From the sergeant's point of view, this kind of got the new officers out of the way, in a manner of speaking. Most of the time the catwalk was not needed anyway, and this would leave the sergeant with more experienced officers on the galleries.

One thing I did like about the catwalk, was the eagle nest view, which would afford me the opportunity to see about ninety-five percent of the cell house, although not necessarily at the same time.

I watched the other officers as they secured and re-secured the unit the entire night. The two things I noticed the most, was that this was what they seemed to be doing the majority of the time; securing or un-securing, and that the officers didn't usually go on the galleries unless absolutely necessary. The galleries seemed to be the domain of the inmates. Going in and out of cells, and back and forth from the shower; the galleries appeared to be the inmate's private retreat.

The officers secured the unit at the beginning of the shift, except for a few doors, which belonged to supposed cell house help. This was a clear violation of ADs* and DRs* but I would soon be groomed just like many before me, to disregard the same observations as well.

While we were waiting for the count to check and while the officers hurriedly went to chow, I had a chance to reflect on my more memorable moments while in H-House.

Other than the few fights, the most memorable thing that happened, had to have been when I was escorting a line to the law library. A few days a week, I escorted anywhere from a half a dozen inmates to upwards of thirty, to the law library, and sometimes alone although this assignment called for two officers. The law library was relatively close at about three hundred yards away. We walked around to the back of the library building, which made it a little longer. Most of the time, at least one of the three south wall towers had us in plain view.

Except for the last few minutes when we were entering the rear of the building, when our view was totally obstructed and we were in one of the blind spots of the institution. Usually two officers escorted the line. On the days when the unit was short officers, and it was, on many occasions, (another violation of AD's and DR's, but who's counting) I would escort the line alone.

I came to the last locked gate right before the rear door of the library. The gate I was going to open to let my line through, had another inmate on the opposite side unescorted. He was dressed in painter's overalls and a hat. He also was pulling a small cart on wheels with several gallons of paint and brushes.

First, I didn't even know who he was, although I had a unwanted clue. Second, he wasn't escorted as I said, and third, he was population and my inmates were not supposed to come in contact with population inmates, for obvious reasons.

So while the inmate is motioning for me to open the gate, and while the P.C inmates are yelling "Hey Rich what's happening?" I started to reach for my radio, when a white shirt happened to wonder by. He told me open the gate, and said, "don't worry, Mr. Speck there is an institutional painter and is on his way back to G-Dorm". Which was an honor dorm for inmates with assignments on the prison grounds or in the Soap Shop, Taylor Shop or Furniture Factory. After I opened the gate, I met Richard Speck an infamous Chicago mass murderer. He of course was cordial about the whole thing, assuring me that "he understood" why I didn't open the gate immediately. On my way back to H-House all I could keep thinking was "MR SPECK"... "MR SPECK".

I wasn't sure if the presence of Richard Speck was the dominating factor, or if it was the fact that this sick ass had free reign in the institution. I wasn't sure if the white shirt referring to him as Mr. had annoyed me, all I know is I remember that night like the back of my hand, and I am sorry to say I will never forget it. He had murdered several nurses in the sixties as mentioned before, for those of you who are lucky enough not to recognize the name, yet a pig (pardon my conviction) like that looked well fed, and totally at ease to say the least. He actually seemed jovial. I guess since he had been here so long, he learned to accept his lot in life, but it still pissed me off.

I asked that white shirt, a few days later how I was supposed to determine the inmates I can assist and the ones I shouldn't. He said, "Don't worry, you'll get to know the one's who have the Visa cards and one's who don't". At that point, I wasn't sure if I really wanted to learn, considering the first example. I also learned that in B-East this "some were allowed, and some weren't" rule applied a lot more than at H-house.

Just then, the horn sounded, indicating a count check and the officers were coming back into the unit from lunch.

My mindset began to return, and I watched closely, as the officers let out the four hundred or so inmates for chow. The other officer on the catwalk had been around a bit longer, and explained that we were supposed to be an equalizer of sorts. As I considered this tidbit, I wondered how this could be possible, four hundred inmates with a myriad of unknown weapons versus five officers on the floor with no weapons, and two on the catwalk with a pistol grip 870 Wingmaster and four rounds of #00 buckshot each. Considering we were supposed to fire a warning shot into the ceiling in the event of an altercation, the simple math says we would be left with 6 or 7 rounds. Depending of course, on whether one officer or two fired warning shots. This comparison or ratio would be brought up on many occasions to the powers that be. All of which, were met with basically the same reply "This is the way it is, DEAL with it!"

Sometimes they would give me some song and dance, on how it was worse in the past. The one I liked the most though, was when they said, "at one time we didn't even have a catwalk, be happy with what you have now"

All along the officers wondered why it was so difficult to add rounds to the catwalk. On one occasion, I saw the warden in the tunnel, and asked if I might have a minute of his time and he said "sure". I thought this was my big moment, somehow believing that logic would most certainly drive the conversation to a productive end. So I asked " Why couldn't more rounds be put up on the catwalk? His reply more or less was " on a few occasions officers had dropped rounds onto the flag, and even the shotgun itself once or twice," and he thought we had enough to deal with. Sensing his displeasure with the lack of professionalism by the past officers I then inquired "why couldn't a strong box of some sort be placed on the catwalk in the backroom on the wall containing a box of shells for emergency purposes only"? This way the incompetent officers wouldn't have a chance to screw up. He then gave me a strange look and said in a very aggravated tone "officer go to your assignment"! So much for my assumed logic!

Well back to the B-East world of thrills and chills. My first shift went relatively smooth, except for a minor altercation at the door. From my vantage point, I couldn't tell what was being said. I did notice as the inmate was arguing with the door officer, he looked up at me. Most likely to see if I was actually there and to ascertain what his options were.

When I returned the following day believe it or not, and I met the real sergeant, Jamie Bigosh. I couldn't get any type of read from his face or demeanor, so I decided I would talk with him later, in hopes of getting to know him. He then assigned me the upper two galleries, known as eight and ten. I had learned that Sergeant Bigosh had just received his sergeant stripes, and this was his first assignment as a sergeant, so I didn't know what to think of his assigning me to the galleries. I could only assume he was trying me out. Over time, I learned to like and respect Sergeant Bigosh very much. Although some of his decisions seemed strange to me, he had been around for ten years and somehow things always seemed to get done in a timely fashion.

The lines from the daily classes or programs were starting to enter the unit and the sergeant handed me the keys for the upper two galleries and said "this man belongs in 1001, think you can handle that?" I went up to the top gallery and 1001 was the first door. As I started to open the door that appeared closed to the naked eye, the inmate grabbed the door and pulled it open. "No key required" he said in a jovial kind of way, and promptly went into the cell closing the door behind him.

At least it appeared closed, it sounded like it closed, and when I yanked on it, it didn't open, and so it must have been closed. So I proceeded back down to the sergeant's office wondering what my next adventure would be. I was going to try my best even though I learned in H-House that this wasn't always the best idea. Before we go any farther, let me try and give you a better mental picture of B-House. The Unit actually had two sides. B-East was only half the building. The building was split long ways, B-East on one side, and B-West on the other. B-West, like B-east had over 400 inmates, with its own set of officers and its own catwalk. They ran completely independent of each other. The two catwalks were actually connected, and it would appear either side could help the other in case of a major disturbance, but technically, the catwalk officers were supposed to stay on their respective sides.

Each unit had five galleries. B-West had the odd number galleries and B-East had the even ones. This should explain the top two galleries on my side being referred to as eight and ten. There was a door each for B-East and B-West heading into the tunnels on the north end of the building on the flag. On the opposite end of the building each unit had a door going to their respective yards. In case of an emergency, there was a fire escape in both units that ran from the top gallery to the flag, centered in the middle of each unit. Also in defense of management, there were several canisters located just above each catwalk, which were rumored to house CS* gas in case of a riot. These were controlled from outside the unit.

I am glad I never had to test the theory. So all in all, B-East and B-West combined, the entire building housed close to nine hundred inmates. Both units B-East and B-West as well as segregation used the same frequency on the radio. Quite often problems occurred due to this "sharing" of frequencies. Many times, a new officer or an idiot would be tying up the radio with some unnecessary bullshit. A major incident would take place, whether it was a fight or a fire in a cell, and it might take several minutes before the message actually got out and the help arrived to assist.

This situation did occur on many different occasions. Some of the repercussions were more severe than others. This state of affairs was also brought up in conversation on many different occasions, only to end in the same old run-around.

We did at one point receive radios that appeared to fix this problem. They had plenty of channels to accommodate all the units. The only problem was we were only testing these for the State Police. The fact they suited our circumstances and the fact we had to give them up after getting used to them, will always remain a mystery to me! These radios even had extension mic's you could connect to your shirt right below your ear. This was a great addition, considering the level of noise in the cell house sometimes. As usual though, the officers woke from the dream.

At this particular point in time, each unit had a door officer, three gallery officers, two catwalk officers and a sergeant. Sometimes, you didn't get that many though. Even though the ADs and DRs made it perfectly clear that this was the minimum compliment of staff allowed. Sometimes the shift captains wanted to look good for the administration, or sometimes the administration wanted to look good for the people in Springfield. Whatever the motivating factor, the amount of overtime was a constant issue in decision-making. Always applying direct pressure on the chances of a unit functioning efficiently. All the while the support staff and front line officers wedged in the middle.

There was a daily draft list the shift captains had at their disposal; in case of too many call-offs. This was a mandatory overtime list actually, and an officer could be written up for refusing. On many occasions the shift captains, were instructed not to draft anyone regardless of the circumstances, or maybe they were limited to a given amount. Whatever the reason, the institution ran short on more occasions than I care to remember. Lets keep in mind again, for the mentally challenged out there; this isn't a fast food restaurant. It isn't about burgers and service to the customers. This is about lives on the line every single day. The administration was more concerned with budgets and looking good for Springfield, regardless of the corners that were cut and regardless of the people that were hurt.

The gallery officers were assigned as follows. One officer had the lower two galleries, one officer was assigned the middle gallery along with the shower, and one officer had the upper two galleries. One officer was assigned the door and then of course, the two on the catwalk.

When I arrived down at the sergeant's office, I inquired as to why the door opened on its own. I did ramble a bit, but I am talking about the door at 1001 that pretty much opened itself. I was informed that more than half the doors in the unit did this, and even more in B-West. The officers told me this was the way it had been for a long time. The funny thing here was the fact that there were locksmiths continually fixing doors, but seemingly getting nowhere.

Sergeant Bigosh told me to go to my galleries, secure them, and then once secured begin my count. An officer did go with me initially, but left shortly thereafter, as he had his own galleries and his own mess to deal with.

Ten gallery the uppermost, was mostly old timers and inmates that worked in the industry* and so the lockup there went relatively easy. I remember thinking, "this isn't so bad," but again it was in fact just a temporary lull in the festivities. Eight gallery on the other hand was a totally different animal. The inmates on this gallery were much younger then the inmates on ten, mostly were new, and unassigned* as well. I would find, that as a rule, I ended up expending triple the time and energy locking up eight gallery as I did on ten gallery.

Ten gallery was mostly single man cells, where as eight was mostly two man cells. The way I was treated between the two galleries was like night and day. Ten gallery inmates virtually secured themselves. For the most part, all I had to do there was check the doors. Since most of the inmates on eight were relatively new, they spent the majority of their time trying to convince their brothers they could deal with prison life. They of course did this in many ways. One of which, was fucking with the guards in any way possible. They knew of course, the newer

47

the guard, the easier to screw him and gain respect from their peers.

As I reflect back again on those times, I do realize, if I was aware of half the stunts pulled on me, I would have probably resigned along time before I actually did. It took a while to learn the usual games, but as each day went by, I became without a doubt more proficient at spotting the bullshit. I continually learned my craft and attained a better understanding of my opponents, but somehow the job didn't get easier. I just ended up with more questions than I had before.

On this first lock-up of the day, I was instructed prior to my going up there, that most of the inmates should be secured in their cells. The only ones I would be expected to lock-up were the ones entering the unit. This as usual was a bunch of horseshit. Ten-gallery in fact was pretty much secured. So I went down to eight. Eight-gallery had between ninety and one hundred inmates assigned at any given time. I would find that the majority of them were on the gallery or running somewhere else in the cell house no matter the day or the time.

As I stood there with my finger up my ass, an officer that was assigned to the lower two galleries came to assist me. I was needless to say, grateful for his presence since I really didn't have a clue who went where and the inmates knew it. (Note for future administrations: nametags with assigned unit and cell numbers mandatory on uniforms, color-coded preferably) As far as I was concerned this gallery would have taken at best two hours to secure.

The officer indicated the proper way was to make a pass on the gallery locking up the inmates that wanted to be locked up (Yup, that's what I said, the ones that wanted to!) Then we would make another pass and lock up the rest. The first pass, according to inmate officer communication was somehow the prelude to the supposed final lock-up. This wouldn't have been the way I would have expected it to get done, but this was the law of the land regardless. Even with my reservations I was pleasantly surprised that about twenty minutes later, the gallery was as secure as it could be. Except for of course the four doors or so, the officer instructed me should stay open because they were phone men. I wondered at this point why it was imperative that phone men where out when it was institutional rules that the phones were shut down during count procedure, and didn't come back on till count check?

When I arrived back at the sergeant's office I asked Sergeant Bigosh if this many inmates were always out when we walked in the door. He replied " Sometimes there are more inmates out than should be; and this wasn't of course the way it should be," and that if I wanted I could write a 434*. According to him, that would do no good anyway, because the 7-3 shift would just say those inmates had just came in the unit as their shift ended, or they must have kicked out of their cells. This would be just another example of the "DEAL WITH IT" mentality.

He also advised me that the 434 would not only be rocking the boat, it was essentially a complete waste of ink. I decided to let it go, and continue to try and learn as much as possible.

I noticed as we descended the stairs that there were inmates out on all the galleries. Even though count procedures were in effect, and even though they had been secured only minutes before. Whoops, another violation of ADs and DRs.

When we were counting my galleries, I came up with a given physical count. The other officer informed me that I should add two inmates to the ten-gallery count, and two inmates to the eight-gallery count to the tally sheets. I of course said, "I prefer not to do that if the bodies are not physically there." He then walked me down to the unit door and showed me approximately ten inmates outside the B-East and B-West unit doors. He explained he knew each inmate out there, and what cell they belonged to. Although they were supposed to have been inside the unit for count and secure, this was a usual modus operandi of Stateville and I shouldn't be bothered by it. I noticed one inmate even had a leather-bound briefcase.

Just then I observed Lieutenant Tomms come out of his office and introduce himself. He said if I had any questions; don't hesitate to talk with him. I recall thinking…He didn't actually realize what he had gotten himself into with that comment. I of course still had to pass out the mail on my galleries and do my paperwork, so the Q and A had to wait.

The counts were supposed to be done by two officers, but sometimes only one counted and the others just signed the count slip. This was a corner cutting technique that was used by all the population units' part of the time. Many officers received write-ups because of this inadequacy as well. You really couldn't blame the sergeant for this. Time restraints and staff shortages almost always dictated yet another curvature in the rules. So I signed to the fact that I had counted all five galleries even though I had only counted the upper two. And even those two weren't precise.

At this point I started to complete my paperwork. There were numerous sheets to fill out along with the many logbooks. The thing here was that each of these sheets and logbooks we were filling out and/or signing, were just another tool for the administration. They knew the officers had no way of completing all these duties. With this, the officers passed them around in a hurried fashion as if just to complete them, and acted as though they had little if any importance.

We then went to chow, two at a time. This left the unit with just one gallery officer for what was supposed to be a half an hour, but seemed like more the better part of an hour. We usually brought trays of food back for the catwalk and sergeant, since with the aforementioned time restraints they rarely had the chance to go themselves.

So much would be made of this managerial inadequacy down the road, that eventually they would have officers that did nothing more then relieve other officers for chow. On this day I ended up going to chow with Officer Jones. He told me, "not to worry about anything, that in time I would begin to feel more comfortable with what was going on." Although I appreciated the pat on the back, I was hoping he didn't really mean that eventually I would become a robot like everyone else ignoring the obvious. I also asked him why we continually ignored the rules, like the doors being left open. He said "it was easier in the long run, because the doors left open were either cell house help, or the cells of inmates that would be coming in the unit the minute the count checked.

When the officers had finished chow, the count had checked and we were instructed to let out the entire house. Are we in a maximum-security cell house or am I mistaking something here? After the house had been totally let out, I couldn't believe my eyes. There were literally dozens of inmates everywhere. Some even came into the sergeant's office uninvited and sat down. They appeared as comfortable as if they were at home with their feet up on the sofa.

Most of the inmates were just milling around. Some were playing cards or chess, while some were in the back of the cell house lifting weights. Note to future administrations: NO free-weights…and preferably put the weight machines in the gym only. Some were busy selling home made wares while others where selling items obviously stolen from the kitchen or elsewhere. The cell house had the feel of a kind of outdoor marketplace.

Finally, the inmates were called to chow. After the chow line was complete, the door officer gave a count to the sergeant. This was the usual procedure, so the sergeant could log the number of inmates that went to chow, in the cell house logbook. This at first glance would seem to be a procedure that would most certainly be utilized in a prison. The inconceivable dilemma here though was this. The door officer was not required to count the line upon its return. So what was the point? What did I know for that matter, a relatively new officer to the prison and a brand spanking new one to the population unit B-East. So again, I shut my mouth and didn't ask questions. The inmates also did not go out in an orderly fashion when fed, like the movies that most of us have seen. They went out at their leisure in small groups, and it took several calls on the cell house intercom to finally get them all out. This was an every day occurrence, asking them to go to chow, as opposed to doing what I thought would be our job, and ordering them to go.

Depending on the evening, chow could last from twenty minutes, to close to an hour. Some meals were more extensive than others, so this wasn't always the system at fault. From about five thirty until approximately nine at night the inmates had the run of the unit. Not to mention the prison proper. Doing the usual… violations, extortion's, gambling, dealing in whatever, and so many more assorted improprieties, it really is a miracle that more people on both sides were not hurt or killed.

The one good thing about the chow time was that I was able to finally talk with Lieutenant Tomms. I stepped in his office and the first order of business was for me to sign several post descriptions, one for each of the posts in the unit, as well as a few others.

I don't hold anything against his requiring this. As you must obviously assume, he didn't make the rules, he was just doing his job. You might also be wondering, what was the problem here? Well, just another way to hook up an officer. The post descriptions were written as, "HOW IT SHOULD BE DONE", in the proper environment. This wasn't the proper environment, and almost none of the information in the post descriptions really applied. So therefore, it would be nothing but paperwork to actually set an officer on the path to the front door, given even a minor insurrection of some sort. So for those slow folks out there, if something went wrong, and often did, the administration could point to your signature and basically stick it up that proverbial place where they say the sun doesn't shine.

You as an officer, had signed and attested to the fact you knew how the job was apparently done, and in the same quick apparently inconspicuous moment, actually signed your resignation. Post descriptions, yea ok... the administration knew as well as we did, life in the cell house was totally different than the fantasy on paper.

Another conundrum; regarding the door assignment itself and the officer assigned, was that YOU as the door officer were required to shake inmates down as they entered the unit. This was a joke actually. A rule; yes it was, enforced; no it wasn't. So if you did attempt to do your job properly, the inmates looked at you like you were nuts. I guess in effect, you actually were crazy. Some officers tried to do the job in the prescribed manner, but most didn't, which meant of course if you were one of the few attempting to do the job correctly, you appeared to be harassing the inmates more or less.

It wasn't the fault of the residents that the security measures were less than consistent and enforced in a haphazard manner. Because of this, the inmates had no problem actually mentioning the officers, sergeants or lieutenant's name that broke the rules and allowed them to take food in the unit on prior occasions. They then of course, would follow that up with the "what's your problem angle?" At the beginning of my stay in B-east this strategy by the inmates actually worked. I was too naive for it not to. It would take a few incidents of embarrassment for me to finally handle the door quandary in the proper manner.

On many occasions, and too many to count I might add, an argument would ensue at the door regarding food entering the unit, and not always ending with the same result. The usual outcome was something to the effect that the food would be thrown away anyway, so might as well let the inmates have it. This of course meant letting them in the unit with the food in question.

Appearing to be another miniscule problem, the food many times would start arguments and to some degree, borderline riots. Food is currency in the prison system, the same as cigarettes, sex, or paper money for that matter. On one shakedown in particular, over a thousand dollars was confiscated from an inmate's radio inside his cell. For all the geniuses in the system that don't understand that concept, allow NO food from the kitchen inside the units whatsoever.

The food the inmates were bringing in of course was going to their chief, or going for debts owed or for drugs or whatever. It was also ALWAYS STOLEN! Rarely, did I see the inmates that brought in the food, eat the food. Now, I did see them selling or bartering the stolen state food quite often during my entire tenure at Stateville.

Again, don't get me wrong, allowing the food (at this point in time) into the unit always calmed the situation, and yes it probably would have been thrown away regardless. That was when it had already been prepared as well. Many times the inmates were caught with entire institutional size portions of foodstuffs. This was as a rule confiscated if stumbled upon by security staff. I of course had mixed emotions regarding this continual daily puzzle. I for one, didn't care either way were the food went.

The rules were the rules though, and again circumvented, as so many other rules before had been. How was I to change understood and accepted illegal practices of so many years on my own? One thought in defense of some of the white shirts; some were very good at what they did, and the food being allowed in the unit, had been going on for a very long time, so I don't really blame them. It's just that some white shirts allowed some things and some didn't. Some allowed milk and juices only. Some didn't allow juices, because it could be used to create hooch*. Some didn't allow chicken or whole trays but some did. Some went as far as to not allow any food, EXCEPT for chiefs or inmates that were spilling their guts concerning the cell house intricacies. Some even gave the direct impression, they didn't want to be bothered, and so the story goes. Some hid behind the bars on their shirts, while others felt the brunt trying to maintain some conformity.

Here again, each shift was different because the compliment of employees was likewise dissimilar. Whiteshirts could bump to other shifts and assignments as well. So, the compliment of whiteshirts not only changed in size but character. I would eventually learn the majority of the brass. The ones I could count on, and the ones that weren't worth the bars on their shirts.

The door to the unit actually consisted of two doors. The area between the two doors was referred to as the interlock. The interlock was of course off limits to residents except during the movement of lines for chow and such. We though, with our some rules apply attitude, allowed inmates in this secure area all the time. It wouldn't have been, but with minimal effort for an inmate or inmates, to have taken the key and effectively had total control of the entire units movement. Since B-East and B-West were side by side, and the interlocks ran horizontal, directly adjacent to each other, the inmates from either side always wanted to converse. We like the imbeciles we were, allowed this daily. Yes, I say we, because I am ashamed to admit, when I use the word we, it did apply. Not that I wanted it that way, it was just that I rather enjoy breathing and drawing other security staff into an already screwed up situation didn't make much sense either.

One incident sticks out very clearly in relation to this malady. I had let an upper echelon inmate, (gang wise)(and authorized by the sergeant) in the interlock, for a supposed few minutes. As I stood there watching him, I observed what appeared to be and a shank sticking out of his sock. Even though my call for assistance went well, and even though the shank was confiscated and the inmate sent to segregation, it's not rocket science to determine potential serious scenarios. The funny thing on design here was that the two interlocks could have been easily and completely separated! Note to future administrations: Separate the interlocks with a few large pieces of sheet metal rather than the metal mesh that's currently present. This was not to be though, at least as long as I was there. Must have been a part of the master plan. A "need to know" basis kind of thing, I guess. With the change of personnel on a daily basis, this normality became a major problem also, just as the food did on a daily basis. Give em' an inch and they will take a mile I suppose.

So along with learning the lieutenants and sergeants that I could trust, I also inadvertently learned the gang chiefs, primarily due to their SPECIAL privileges. I also began to learn some of the gang's rosters as well. This was because they left the unit for the most part as a group.

The door also had a list of inmates that were allowed to exit the unit for tunnel jobs, such as sweeping and mopping. The thing here is inmates might loose their job for whatever reason and their name would remain on these lists. Thus allowing them access to the tunnels and the adjoining cell houses anyway. Sometimes the wrong inmates would end up in the wrong unit. This of course, was not by accident. All they had to do was enter with a chow line, when the door officer was relatively new, or at least new to that particular unit. Many of the assaults could be directly attributed to the security problems at the different unit doors.

An inmate could enter with one line and leave with another. Entering the unit, doing his dirty work (whatever that was) and leave undetected! I remember a female officer that lost her job; because she allowed an inmate to enter the wrong unit and he assaulted an inmate in that unit. Yes, she was wrong, and deserved to loose her job. With that in mind though, three quarters or more of the staff should have been fired as well. The difference being, no rules appeared to have been broken on those many other occasions. So whatever works I guess.

My first day on the door went as expected really. I wasn't really doing anything but opening and closing the door. The list on the door had been scratched out and erased so many times, I had to ask the sergeant or the lieutenant pretty much each time an inmate wanted out or in. I am ashamed to admit it, but it didn't take very long before I was part of the problem. All I could hope for was that I, like the female previously mentioned, didn't get caught up in a gargantuan mess. When a sergeant or lieutenant told me to let a given inmate out that I wasn't sure should be out in the first place, I had a few options. Question it, write a report, or let him out. The only thing at Stateville that was cut and dry was that nothing was cut and dry. Sometimes inmates had temporary jobs that maybe the brass was only aware of. So if you did question something, you usually would end up with an ear full. You know the argument… "Don't question my authority I just gave you and order kind of thing." Sure I could write something down on my clipboard stating so and so was authorized to be out. Then that superior amnesia thing would rear its ugly head. The "he said, she said kind of thing."

The main thing I was beginning to gain knowledge of was to recall the so-called important inmates and the brass that attempted to go by the rules. Actually it was safer to some extent with the brass that didn't go by the rules. Partially because the rules had been circumvented for so long this was obviously a much smoother avenue.

Another story comes to mind of an officer that was brand spanking new. This was his first day and the brains decided the door was a good spot for him. He had been instructed that no food comes in the unit. He was a plain, simple "English is English" type. Totally unaware of all the URs (unwritten rules), which could only be learned by experience and trial and error, he attempted to do exactly as instructed. I happened to be on the catwalk that day. This officer, whom I will refer to as "Officer Porkchop" had the door. The line was returning from the evening meal and my job basically consisted of watching the door officer, while trying to ensure a small degree of safety. Officer Porkchop was watching the line enter, when one of the Latin Disciples, who happened to have the last bite of a porkchop in his mouth, came walking through the door. It was literally the last bite of that porkchop, and it appeared the inmate was about to throw the food in the garbage can, when out of the blue;

Officer Porkchop snatches the bone from the inmate's grasp and tosses it into the garbage can himself. The inmate with his survival mentality, smacks open handedly, the officer across the face. Pretty much in unison the chow line stopped cold turkey, and I put a warning round in the ceiling, and then immediately leveled the weapon on the inmate that assaulted the officer. This was the inmate's only warning; and he knew the next sound wouldn't be a good one. So everything switched into a large verbal confrontation.

Several whiteshirts and officers came from the tunnel area to assist. More than a few inmates had stopped around the area of the door, most of those LDs* of course, while several other inmates lined up on the stairs to the different galleries. Since the inmate assaulted the officer, his departure from the unit would be automatic. Since according to the inmates the situation shouldn't have occurred in the first place, several inmates took to chanting derogatory phrases while trying to incite a more dangerous situation. Due to the fact the stairs and door were both blocked by a couple hundred inmates, the residents that wanted to get to their cells and stay out of the way couldn't, and this only enhanced the severity of the situation. The cuffing of the inmate proved to be a delicate situation, as the rest of the inmates protested rather loudly.

Luckily, all went well, and the inmate found his way to I-House (segregation) and we eventually secured the unit. And all of this; over a little piece of porkchop. The inmate was given three months in segregation for the assault. He would end up with less then thirty days due to overcrowding and the mitigating circumstances. WHAT mitigating circumstances? Inconsistent management was the only mitigating circumstances that I could see! Just another example of why the rules should have been enforced all along. The shame here is, no one was wrong. The inmate had done this exact thing countless times before, and the officer was doing what he was told to do. The administration too, was behaving as they always did. The inmates were so used to lax security they had started confusing privileges with rights. This situation too could have ended a lot differently, and was just another example of administration circumventing the rules of the road.

Somewhere, Officer Porkchop is doing his job, because the administration there, allow him to. Actually, if I was a lawyer, I could argue each side, but what would be the point, this was Stateville justice at its finest!

Get something to drink if you're thirsty because I'm getting back on the soapbox for a moment. There were basically three entities at Stateville; the staff, the administration, and the inmates. At any given point, any combination of the three could be friend or foe. One minute, one of those entities could help you or they could effectively hurt you. Let me give a few examples.

After I had been at the 'Ville a short while, some of the inmates began to confide in me to certain degrees. I don't claim to know if this was because they liked or respected me or if I just started to blend into their usual setting or routine. Either way I became familiar with several residents and sometimes they would tell me on the QT that something was about to happen. Not necessarily all the facts mind you, but to just watch my back.

More often than not, these became some of my most reliable tidbits of information I would receive from any source. So sometimes the inmates actually appeared to be my friends. As for some of the officers, they sometimes became MIA when shit hit the fan. And as such, sometimes it appeared they weren't my friends. The administration of course was like a roulette wheel, always seeming to land on the color or number you of course had not bet on. So the administration was usually perceived as foe.

Well let me see…the prison did have some good points. The walls did their job 99% of the time, so at least the inmates remained inside and were not walking the streets. It also gave people employment, as seemingly unnecessary as those jobs may have seemed. It served as a home away from home for the unfortunate that had previously lived in already dysfunctional situation.

With all the strange and negative vibrations emanating from the place, a person with a warped, or in the process of being warped, sense of humor could find plenty to laugh about. It was the devils playground, a homosexual's paradise; a con mans heaven, a derelicts utopia. Humor could be found at all levels, but maybe that was the beginning of a defense mechanism some didn't understand. At least the one's with some sense of right and wrong in the first place. Not attempting to state that my humor was of the normal type from the start, but I do think over time, I too fell victim to the warped humor that plays havoc with my internal workings to this day. I find myself laughing about things, I know a dozen or so years ago wouldn't have been the least bit funny.

Another moniker of the juiced up inmate (no pun intended), was an assortment of jewelry. None of which was issued by the state, and some necklaces so large, an officer could take an elaborate vacation if he owned same. NO, I wasn't jealous, I was pissed off. Inmates walking past the administration with enough gold wrapped around their necks to start a small jewelry store. Earrings were also against the rules, but the inmates wore them anyway. Usually directly in reference to which side of gangland they played in.

Confronting the inmates about this infraction as usual didn't make sense, since it had been the norm for too long to mention. "Cardinal rule" for future administrations, don't give something, or allow something, that you know eventually you will have to take back... Did someone say common sense?

I remember very clearly, when a memorandum was passed down the shit pile. It very emphatically stated more or less " from this point on, earrings of any type would not be tolerated". Of course, they were expecting the front line security to enforce it. This irritated the shit out of me. I could potentially get a write up, and loose pay if I didn't confront an inmate doing three life terms about a silly fucking earring, he had been allowed to have all along. Pardon the vernacular, emotions again. One thing in defense of the author's loose tongue, I learned how to express myself in many different ways while employed at Stateville. As you can see, some have been hard pressed to fade away.

Yes, I do believe for the most part the earrings were eliminated, but if you have been reading and paying attention, that wasn't the problem. Ramble as I might, I can't help but give numerous examples of how a complete waste of effort doing this job actually was.

I found humor in the inmate picnics or banquets. It was of course good for inmate morale', and relieved tension I assume. Yet this too, was just another example of a privilege turned into a right. It seemed from my vantage point, that inmate comfort was of primary concern to the powers that be. Obviously from a security standpoint, state of mind of the populace as a whole, is very important. It's just that the comfort factor continually grew. Whenever I saw one of the wardens and there were three, no analogy intended (Moe, Larry, and Curly), they were always surrounded by an entourage' of inmates. I have to admit, if I was in that environment and had a problem, I too would probably go to the top and avoid the riff raff in between. It appeared from a layman's eyes that the wardens and a few of the inmates were like best friends. Body language speaks volumes. I don't confess to be an authority on language of any type, but when pats on the back are exchanged and the inmate is wearing ten pounds of gold followed by a half dozen of his brothers as security, you just have to sit back and say HUH! Well, so much for the pulpit, lets head back to Stateville and enjoy in our own way, another tidbit of infamy.

As stated earlier locking up a gallery took a certain amount of finesse'. You had basically two options here. You could be the hard guy type, locking up everything in your path, or you could use a combination of child psychology and negotiation tactics. Since negotiation is so much like bargaining, that seemed like the tool of choice, I chose the later. I decided I would treat an individual exactly how he treated me, regardless of his affiliations. The inmates at first were somewhat put off, but seemed to slowly conform to how I approached them. There are a few things I actually enjoyed about the job. Conquering the galleries in my own way, was without a doubt the pinnacle. My stature was a major contributor in my limited options either way. In all walks of life, there are always a few that buck the system no matter what. Here being no different, in that respect. Some inmates didn't give a shit if you threw them in the cell, or you talked to them like human beings, they were not going to lock up till you had a coronary or a whiteshirt came to assist. I guess that's why, they were where they where, in the first place.

If all else failed I had an ace in the hole. It was a neat little item known as a disciplinary report. If an inmate refused to lockup I could "write a ticket". This, I would have to equate with firing rubber bands at eagles. The ticket had little power, little intimidation, and at best, relayed to the inmate in question, that you in fact knew how to write, and were disgusted. Sure they had commissary denial applied. No commissary, what a crock!! All this did was open the door for loan capitalists. If in fact your cell wasn't already filled to the brim with excess amounts of commissary to begin with.

I remember getting a kick out one of the disciplinary reports I had written though, and the story goes something like this… One particular time, the inmates were going to law library and leaving the unit in their usual straggling way. When one inmate, who on more then one occasion, had a hard time finding his cell in time, decided he would try and impress his brothers. " Ya' know that ticket you gave me Thomas?" I said "Yes what about it?' he said "you can stick it up your ass! I then replied, " The one you get tomorrow, you can stick up yours". Maybe you would had to have been there to totally grasp the timely humor, but the incident remains in my memory to this day.

I was starting to think that as bizarre as my job was, I was starting to get the hang of it. Non-conformity seemed to be the median here, so I tried to use that as my vehicle of representation. Any way I could, to freak out the inmates seemed a good idea. This was a tool they used as well so it obviously was the weapon of choice. So in essence it was a constant tug of war trying to keep each other off balance.

Yet another story regarding the tickets and how to use them strategically comes to mind. I was assigned two-gallery, which housed most of the cell house help. Now this group of individuals actually did have something to loose and as such didn't enjoy receiving tickets very much. Not only were they allowed out before the regular population, and not only were they allowed to stay unsecured longer then the standard populace, but they made a small wage as well. Miniscule as it was, the income combined with the extra movement, and the minor prestige of having a cell house job, made them have to conform more then most.

On this day, the few Latin Disciples on the back of the gallery decided it was "Fuck with Officer Thomas" day. After several attempts to lock up the inmates mentioned, I decided a ticket for each and every one was the way to go. As they ran around the flag like court jesters, I sat in the sergeant's office and wrote each one a ticket of his very own. They even had the gall to come to the sergeant's office after I had been in there like forty-five minutes and ask what I thought I was doing? I explained to them the best I could that I had attempted to come to a meeting of the minds on several different levels and this was my only option remaining.

The next day they had received their tickets and I was again assigned two-gallery. As I walked the gallery, I noticed that every inmate from the day before was in his cell. I thought maybe a cramp in their cigarette flow might be the trick. Hit em' where it hurts, the wallet. Tickets were a crapshoot anyway. One day I could write a ticket and an inmate get thirty days commissary denial. The next day I could write another inmate a report for the exact same infraction and it might be thrown out. I continued writing tickets anyway because I had stock in the "Bic" pen company.

The following day I again was assigned the same gallery. They must have had a little discussion, because this time I had a little surprise. As I arrived at the end of the gallery a few of the inmates had broomsticks in their hands. Being cell house help, this would seem a given. This time though, the inmates were holding the sticks a bit different and had smiles on their faces. All along coaxing me to come closer because it was time for me to lock them up. They made it perfectly clear the tickets I had written were a complete waste of time and didn't bother them in the least. The broomsticks should have bothered me, but I figured if I didn't face them today, there was always tomorrow. I conveyed to them with the best humorous face I could muster that I had a job to do, and regardless of their motivation, I was going to do it! Those inmates and I came to a weird sort of respect, or maybe just a pleasant way to co-exist. I learned from this, that sometimes actions don't always have an equal and opposite reaction. At least at the 'Ville they didn't.

Reflecting, I don't think I ever tested my so-called authority again in such a free wheeling manner. I believe that the mixture off bullshit that I had already experienced had culminated into a kind of precipice of sorts. On this day, I should either try and make it work, or choose another vocation.

Actually, the inmates taught me more about the environment and survival in general then my fellow employees and the administration combined. The teaching of course came inadvertently, to say the least, but at least it was realistic. There were, and I am sure still are, a lot of good people at Stateville. I feel the need to mention this fact, and might feel the need to do it again before the final chapter is written, if only for my own selfish satisfaction. The words printed here are pretty derogatory, and I will leave it up to the readers and players to determine who is who in that relation. The good ones know who they are, as well as the less then good.

I did work with several crews in B-East, most of which where "stellar" to say the least. Considering the continually revolving outside forces, always at work, I am eternally grateful to those I worked with, partially because on a warped level, we all ate a portion of the same shit sandwich. Most all the officers had advice and perceptions of the way things should be, its just that people did their jobs so differently, it was hard to take literally anything said, because it really couldn't be put into play from a practical point of view. The angle one officer took to complete his job, could mean disaster for another attempting the same angle.

The "Hard Guy" types did little in the way of conversing with the inmates. They attempted to do their job mostly by the book, and didn't attempt to get to know anyone on a personal basis. To the complete contrary, where the "negotiator" types. Officers that really attempted to talk to, and understand the inmates. I of course, fell into the category of negotiator. I did though, make it well known, I had my proverbial line in the sand.

Since the entire unit was un-secure for lengthy periods of time, the way you carried yourself was of the utmost importance. Not only being able to carry yourself in an authoritative manner, but to seem to have some semblance for fairness. If the inmates for whatever reason determined or decided you were unfair, you were sunk before you began sailing. We had one officer that played hard guy from the minute he walked into the door. The inmates were constantly on him in one way or the other. He was even accused of spitting in inmates food. Now I don't believe he did that, but because he was such a hard ass the inmates knew the rumor was good enough for him to have some difficulties of his own on the galleries. This was their way of getting some payback.

The way you carried yourself had a direct bearing on how the other officers were treated as well. Some of the hard guy types would tend to be a bit sadistic in the method of operation, so the inmates responded in kind. This sometimes caused extreme levels of aggressiveness between both groups. The negotiator types could easily put a lighter mood in the cell house as a whole, but if you had to many of these types in one unit, the inmates sometimes confused the negotiating with kindness, and kindness with weakness. On the selfish side, I appreciated a officer or two on the hard guy track. This facilitated my angle working to the n'th degree. If the prison had been run like a real prison, and the inmates locked up the majority of the time, the art of effective dialogue would not have played such an integral part. As it was, and from my point of view, If you couldn't, didn't, or just plain wouldn't communicate with the residents, your road was most assuredly going to end on Misery Avenue.

Some of the crews I worked with, attempted to maintain a small amount of solidarity, at least in our little world. If a new officer showed up, with all his preconceived notions of the rules (just like I had at one time), we immediately went into our "do it our way or the highway mode". I think somewhere in this area I started to become part of the monster. For one thing I was beginning to advocate "Our Way", although practical, not proper. I remember us having one group that worked extremely well together. The house was running like a clock and the inmates were becoming a bit perturbed at our effectiveness. Well the inmates happen to observe that we were all white and decided this was the way to split us up. They went to the wardens and claimed we were writing to many tickets and that some of the officers were actually racists. Well the administration of course nodded their little heads and did exactly as they were instructed. That group would not see another week together.

Officer Highlosser comes to mind. Fresh out of the marines, rules and propriety written all over him, he brought an inmate to the sergeant's office. In Officer Highlosser's hand was a hook to assist in opening the already broken doors. Granted, totally illegal, but the inmate was going ballistic, due to the fact that half the cell house owned one anyway, and why should Officer Highlosser pick on him. I think this was where I started drinking on a nightly basis after work. I was torn, the officer was right, the inmate wrong, but the environment dictated letting the inmate go with a verbal warning. I told Highlosser not to write a ticket and just confiscate the hook, knowing full well, the inmate would have a new one in a matter of minutes. I apologize totally to officer Highlosser for my actions that day. Politically correct, and still wrong, I would do the same thing today given the same situation and environment.

The main thing to do as an officer was to learn the officers around you. Everyone had his or her own patterns and peculiarities. I know I have my share. It didn't matter the race, sexual orientation, or age. In the same boat together, all was equal, and our futures depended on each other. Integrity was personal and yet public. Having to watch each other's back was definitely an equalizer. If you didn't watch me today, how do you know I would watch you tomorrow? It's pretty plain to see, it was important to make the work portion of our lives a level playing field with a minimum of personal conflict.

Yet, some officers chose to throw integrity to the wayside. Bringing in contraband, fraternizing with the convicts in a less then professional way, or even in the worse case scenario, having allegiance as a member of a gang literally, unbeknownst to the administration.

At the risk of sounding chauvinistic, I had my reservations about working with females in this environment. We were in charge of grown men, having little if any relations with the opposite sex. Barring the so-called visiting room, which we will laugh about later. Several women during my time at Stateville lost their jobs due to sexual liaisons with inmates. These inmates had nothing but time to figure out ways to beg, borrow, and steal sympathy. They were rather adept at selling themselves in many other ways as well. Some female officers could handle it, some couldn't.

There were for the sake of argument, some female officers that I had the pleasure to have worked with. On many occasions I felt more at ease walking a gallery with one of them, then a number of the male counterparts. Fairness and effectiveness went a long way here, regardless of gender.

The most memorable negative example (followed by the most positive) was that of a new officer. For the sake of anonymity, let's call her Officer Twoface. Officer Twoface was what I thought at first to be an extremely effective officer. She was slightly hyperactive (the author doesn't have too much room to talk), and as such was better then average on the galleries. Which movement on the fast side is an absolute needed ingredient for effective control. She was fun, but serious on the gallery and could lock up a gallery as effectively as anyone, bar none. My first impression capabilities must have been a bit on the shy side because I felt the need to take her under my wing and teach her MY way. We became what I thought were good friends. I also felt pretty good about the fact she was adept at her job and I trained her from the ground up. I also need to mention she was the lone officer that did respond to the story about the old man being stabbed in the neck on the flag. I liked her very much both as an officer and a person. Yet there were officers that had their reservations about her. I couldn't for the life of me understand what caused their suspicions.

Officer Hayward seemed to have the most negativity regarding her job integrity. He told me on many occasions not to trust her, and that he wouldn't himself as far as he could throw her. He said he couldn't as they say "put his finger on it but". He said he just felt she had some hidden agendas and the officer's safety was not her primary concern, although it escaped him as to why he felt he knew this. Several derogatory statements came from inmates regarding officer Twoface as well. I wrote them off as attempts to split our solidarity, when maybe I should given it the same credence as when they told me something was up in the unit.

You see, I had witnessed so many useless officers come through the doors and then return the same way they came in, that I refused to accept that Officer Twoface was a dirty officer. I just plain didn't want to see it!

During this time frame, Officer Hayward was working the catwalk quite often. He had the bird's eye view, with the opportunity to view the majority of the unit. This in itself should have been enough circumstantial evidence. Even though the green uniform Officer Twoface was wearing assisted in the camouflage of sorts. The uniform, the job she was doing, and my flawed perceptions, hid the majority of her unfolding stupidity.

One night during an apparently routine shift, Officer Twoface called me to the officer's bathroom via the radio. Through the door I asked, "What was the problem? She then in a very low and shaky voice said she was having female problems and that she should be out in a few minutes. She said she just wanted to let me know she was ok, because she already had been in there a while, and that she should be out shortly. Well shortly didn't happen. She called me back to the door about ten minutes later and asked for the medical personnel. At this point I was really confused. The med-techs ended up taking her out of the unit and to the hospital. The weird thing is they had to find some pants for her to wear. When I entered the bathroom after she had been taken out of the unit, her underclothes and here uniform pants were soaked with blood. I wasn't ever privy to the events of that day, but I am sure they had something directly to do with the affair she was having with one of the unit chiefs. I'd rather not comment any further.

The inmates were trying to convey to me that she was dirty, especially inmates from gangs other than the chief's that she was having the affair with. The inmates have a direct view of the bottom galleries because of a reflection coming off the windows, below the catwalk. They can actually look from ten gallery and see pretty much see everything going on five galleries below on the flag.

What actually happened was Officer Twoface, came into work on one of my off days. She was passing the first couple gates, heading to the cell house, and internal affairs met here and escorted her to the internal affairs office. She was in the process of bringing contraband into the prison in here shoe. She was having some serious problems with this chief and here affair was going sour. So she thought that she would recruit one of the local thugs to actually kill the chief in question.

Little did she know that this inmate known as "Ugly" in the cellhouse had no intentions whatsoever to kill anyone. He was in the midst of a lengthy sentence and was smart enough to realize that if he served up an officer to Springfield, he could negotiate a change in venue as well as a reduction in time served. Officer Twoface was actually talking with this inmate from here home by telephone. It is common knowledge that the phones in the prison are monitored. Maybe not all of them, all the time, but monitored none the less.

The Internal Affairs Division was taping the conversations and knew when she was going to be bringing in the contraband. The events transpired over a long period, so the state had time to set up the case. So referring to officer Twoface as less then clever is the politically correct way to refer to her.

I would never really find out the exact agreement between Ugly and the state, but I did notice his rapid departure after turning in Officer Twoface. As for Officer Twoface, she served a little over two years in Dwight Correctional Center; a female prison located in the center of the state.

One last reference to this incident; apologies go out to Officer Hayward, as he was right on target regarding the integrity of the aforementioned officer. The really amazing thing is the first thing an officer learns, is not to trust the inmates. They have nothing but time, to figure out ways to buck the system. Ugly reminded me of a fisherman off the coast of Florida, hoping for the catch of his life. Just like magic, a marlin hits the line, "the suitable for mounting type". Well I guess we all make are own beds and as such have to live with the repercussions of our actions. Considering, that Officer Twoface had about as much brains as a fish, I would have to say the story ended, as it should have. In defense of the officer, I would like to say, "If the prison hadn't run so open in the first place, this scenario might not have taken place. Although she did receive everything she had coming.

A note to current and future officers: Do your eight hours the best you can and get the fuck out. DON'T mess with the inmates. Playing with the inmates isn't worth it. I personally knew two other female officers that had relations with inmates, but we will dispense with the particulars of those situations.

I did have the privilege of knowing and working with several great female officers. One female officer in particular comes to mind, who seemed to always be there when the shit hit the fan. I could always count on her during my entire time at Stateville.

As an indication of her integrity and loyalty to her job, I have one example. I am fighting with an inmate in a cell and trying to get a call over the radio. The next thing I know, she is diving on top of this guy and assisting me in restraining him. She wasn't even assigned my gallery of course but was just keeping an eye on other officers. She also helped me on countless other occasions of varying degrees but enough said. To my knowledge she is there to this day, striking a blow against all opponents of women in men's prisons. Kudos goes out to her, and she knows whom she is.

I know your missing the soapbox somewhat (or did I actually get off) so here it is. I feel for all officers, since they watch these derelicts day in and day out. This is enough stress in itself. The "let them run policy" that the administrations seemed to embrace took its toll on too many officers to count, and in a million different ways.

In a failed attempt to argue for the front office, I don't want to believe that they wanted things as they were, its just that when you give something to someone and then attempt to take it back, your going to most certainly end up with some resistance. Depending on what you're trying to take back in the first place, will probably determine the resistance encountered. An example would be this: I give an inmate a cigarette, and then go and ask for it back. Provided he hasn't smoked it already, he is at least going to argue a minute on why he should have to give the cigarette back. This example is for the sake of simplicity. Why would I give it to him in the first place if I were going to ask for it back? Well at Stateville this applied to the inmates being literally handed the entire prison. The inmates had been given the prison, speaking figuratively at least. They had direct control of day-to-day operations. Eventually the state would see this and attempt to take back the prison.

The inmates are dangerous enough, without adding the element that they felt they were wronged in some way. Eventually policies would have to change, and the inmates and officers would pay. As the entities that put those policies in effect, sat back and absorbed the repercussions in a secondary unaffected way, others felt the mistakes in a more personal and direct way. If something major did occur at the prison, the administration usually gave the press a lot of bureaucratic mumbo jumbo designed to satisfy the masses. I saw this when it slipped out that the doors to the cells were broken and had been for an extended period. The warden of the time actually had the gull to straight up lie and say "the doors are not inoperative". Of course we the public believed him, and why wouldn't we, he is the warden!

Here is just one example of the doors not working properly that thank god ended favorably. The door to B-East consisted of two doors controlling the interlock. There was also a solid door that was to be used in the case of a major insurrection. The door was always left open, partially due to fact that it was common knowledge the door, if secured, would not open again with out the assistance of a locksmith. Most officers were aware of the door and knew that several work orders had gone neglected. Well on this day, a new female officer was being harassed on the door and decided she would secure this door, effectively shutting off the inmate banter. Once she realized she couldn't reopen the door she got on the radio and conveyed this to the sergeant of the unit. The inmates being always in earshot of the officers radios overheard the transmission and just joked and laughed about the security at Stateville. This situation was resolved, and the door was reopened, but the reader can only imagine the potential for disaster.

Things do break and need repair, but this door had been ignored for way to long; just another snafu on the part of the State.

I know that you the reader are probably thinking, something could have been done if the paperwork was given to the proper person. This concept is so wrong it sickens me, because I at one time felt the exact same way. The joint had run fucked up for so long and getting worse that the administration didn't really know where to begin to repair the physical and functional damage. They were in effect just trying to run it the way it was, and praying their erratic situation didn't blow up on them. As you may have seen some officers tried to second-guess their actions on many occasions, but always ended up looking as though we were just stirring up trouble.

Ok maybe, just maybe, the front office didn't exactly cause some of the problems themselves, but they did nothing or very little to effect those problems in a positive productive manner. So they were guilty after the fact on many occasions as well.

I thought at one time, that bringing problems to the attention of the right person would be a good thing to do. When I wrote a couple dozen work orders for doors on two gallery alone, the administration not only didn't appreciate it, they called me on the carpet and asked what I thought I was doing. GIVE ME A

BREAK!! The warden of operations made it clear, that I had actually black balled myself, because those work orders were going to stay in the files. He also accused me of trying to jump on a bandwagon of another employee unhappy with the day-to-day operations. All that officer was trying to do was get a light fixed so she wasn't loading a shotgun in the dark.

By the way, this warden was security at one time, which confused me even more. You would think being security at one point he would understand an officers plight. I guess there is a kind of metamorphosis that takes place when ya' go from security to administration. Your right of course, this book is written by a very disgruntled employee. The officers were getting the shaft so many different ways, that anyone with a full deck can see being disgruntled in this environment wasn't only an eventuality, it was for some, a sick pain that grew continually in the pit of their stomach.

Why, you might ask "did I stay for eight years if things were so bad?" I ask myself that very question often. All I can conclude is I'm stubborn and, or was, an optimist to boot. It was like a monstrous puzzle that took the entire eight years to complete. The picture is fairly clear now, or at least as clear as it will ever become.

Stepping off the soapbox and going back to the Ville' another problem stands out from the rest. The one-thing B-East never had was air-conditioning. Many times during the summer, the cell house was well over one hundred degrees. The good news, or what I thought was the good news, was that the unit had a water fountain that seemed to provide the coldest water in the world. I also felt privy because the B-West and F-House didn't have a water fountain in the unit. Maybe it just seemed so cold because the heat and humidity of the unit would kick your ass.

Well anyway, the water fountain was there for at least two summers during my time there. I drank from it on countless occasions. After they had taken the water fountain out of the unit, of which I was displeased, I read a statement from a lawsuit levied against the state concerning the purity of the water. An independent testing facility had determined that the water that was drank by all concerned, had excessive levels of lead, microscopic worms and excessive levels of radium. Maybe this had something to do with my increasing stomach problems and symptoms of chronic fatigue. The prison was fairly old and the infrastructure antiquated to say the least but, nonetheless, again the powers failed to intercede.

I also found it a bit humorous when at the Springfield Training Academy, we were told that working for Illinois was a definite feather in your cap if you went to another state and worked in their correctional department. I just wasn't clear on whether it was because Illinois was such an exceptional example of corrections in action, or if it was because, if you as an officer could put up with this shit, you could obviously put up with anything! Maybe it was a combination of the two.

Another serious health hazard comes to mind. During my last two years at Stateville I observed what appeared to be an expedited attempt at removing asbestos located throughout the prison and most notably from the pipes in the B-East sergeants office. This locale was my home for about four of my eight-year tenure. This was one of the many added benefits the officer received. Several officers had written work orders years before complaining about asbestos falling from the pipes and being exposed. I had asbestos on my uniform on a few occasions. When I first arrived at the prison, the officer's kitchen was located in a lower level. Along the heating units holding the food, ran pipes designed to steam heat the food using hot water. Those pipes for a period had asbestos around them as well. At the end of this kitchen's life the asbestos was exposed.

Several years ago, they allowed Hollywood to come in to the maximum security prison itself, and film. This partnership has in fact occurred on many occasions. During the filming of one of these movies, an inmate found his way out of the prison using the identification of one of the movie personnel. I am a movie buff, but certain locales should be off limits to filming. For the sake of the idiots in Springfield, ONE OF THESE LOCALES IS A MAXIMUM SECURITY PRISON. Note to future administrations: NO more movies folks; use some common sense! Since Hollywood, does have the capabilities to create whatever environment they want, the partnership on these occasions was about business and business alone.

The problem here is that the state uses corrections and profit interchangeably. The focus is not on the correctional end, but on the bottom line. Obviously, soap and furniture were not paying the way, so they had to think of other avenues. All of course, without a thought about security ramifications. That simply is the mindset in Springfield. For those in the capital that are confused, corrections is simply a deficit and not a profitable venture. Live with it!

The summer that I observed the filming, the personnel involved in the movie were constantly in close proximity to the inmates. This is so ludicrous, I can't find the words to explain the feelings I had. Oh yes, some officers were actually allowed to play bit parts in the filming. So were inmates for that matter, Maximum-security inmates; what a joke. I still wonder why they were surprised, while filming a riot scene, an actor had his jaw broken by an inmate!

The filming of this particular movie took an entire summer. I am not talking about coming into the prison for a day or two. Which in this volatile environment would still be wrong mind you. I'm talking day after day for several weeks. There were trucks used for power stations, cable running everywhere, people roaming everywhere, a buffet set up for actors, the whole nine yards. In defense of the powers that allowed this fiasco, they did stop using inmates at this point. I need to ask you the reader for a favor now, stop me from laughing it hurts!

Several different movies have been made at Stateville; just do some research to see which ones. I talk about money being the prime objective for the administration and the state. Let me give you another example. When the institution would go on lockdown, it would be for an undetermined time usually. The whole institution would not come off lockdown at the same time. The Industry workers were the first to come off, and sometimes two weeks or more ahead of the general population. Ok you say what is the point? MONEY! The industry workers make soap, clothing and furniture. Some of which was sold or used by other prisons. If the inmates are locked up they aren't making items. If they're not making items, they're not making the state money... Simple.

The administration might argue that they let a few inmates out at a time and in increments, for security purposes. That's a bunch of horseshit! If that were the case, they could let out religious services first. The point being, business is business, and corrections is corrections. For the sake of the majority and not the minority please separate the two! The information contained in these pages is more than likely pissing off a lot of people, but as they say, the truth hurts.

During my time at Stateville there were four wardens. The first three were like the stooges. The fourth was sent to clean up the mess of the other three and possibly of others before, of that I don't know. As of my resignation, he was attempting that feat. I am not sure if he ever succeeded, but as of this writing there is already another warden I really do wish him well.

The first warden was Moe; who seemed at first glance, good for the job. I did not understand corrections at all in the beginning, so inmates running everywhere seemed normal at the time. (Only kidding) After sizing up the first administration by action and deed, I decided it couldn't get any worse. This also would prove to be incorrect. The second, Larry, went to the other extreme and tried to play hardball with the inmates, but since Springfield wasn't ready for this turnaround, he didn't last long. The third warden Curly, liked phrases like "weapons free environment" and "open door policy". The problem here was that the door was open all right, but to inmates not officers. He also liked the phrase "Isolated Incident", of which this book derives its name, although I added an "S" for obvious reasons. By Curly's logic this phrase was supposed to have had a calming effect on people when something went down. Making us believe incidents that happened had no relevance to each other whatsoever. Ninety percent of anything that happened at Stateville had a direct link to something else. Most killings were sanctioned*by the inmates in one-way or another. And either the inmates or the powers sanctioned most other actions as well.

The quickest way for an inmate to get killed was to do something major that was not sanctioned and caused a long-term lockdown. This of course put a cramp in the gang's moneymaking ventures and effectively the inmate that had caused the lockdown was like a dead man walking, for lack of a better analogy. Well anyway in my opinion, by the time the fourth warden came along, he couldn't fuck up if he tried. The place had been miss-managed in so many ways, that the only direction was up!

An example of quick and decisive action by the gangs was this little ditty. Once upon a time, there was this homosexual in B-East. He, it, she…whatever, was satisfying everyone in the prison including the chiefs. The sissy failed to mention the fact that he, it, she…whatever, had A.I.Ds (Acquired Immune Deficiency syndrome). The chiefs found out by way of the prison infirmary and shortly after that, the wicked ole' witch was dead. This story was just to break the seriousness.

Back to Curly and his policies. On many occasions I saw inmates going in and out of his office. I saw him walking down the tunnel one day and asked if he had a minute. I of course felt he could spend a minute with an employee seeing how he spent what seemed like hours with residents. He uninterestingly stated "he had half a minute" and clearly gave me the impression he didn't want to spend that much time on any thing I had to talk about regardless of what it was. I could easily see where his priorities stood, but I drove on. I asked him about the many banquets on the yard he was allowing, and his reply was more or less, it's for the benefit of everyone. Yea, ok...explain that to the superintendent that tried to stop a large batch of stolen food from entering the south yard on one of these so called beneficial banquets. He received a quick ass whipping for his efforts!

On the weapons free environment thing, his philosophy as stated at roll call was that "the inmates and the staff could co-exist in harmony". OH Brother, and I thought I was the optimist!

Another of my favorite things to discuss was the mail system in the prison. Each unit received a mailbag usually loaded with mail during the 3-11 shift. The officers were supposed to sort the mail and distribute it. Keep in mind we had over four hundred inmates in our unit. We were also supposed to ask for picture identification from each and every inmate we gave mail to. Sure you could remember some of the faces if you had been around long enough. The problem here was the population was constantly changing, so fresh meat came in every day. It was literally impossible to do this job along with your other responsibilities. Inmates were constantly complaining they hadn't received their mail or another inmate had accepted it.

Of course I believe the inmates should get mail, it's just that this system is without a doubt as ludicrous as it gets. A note for future administrations: A central dispersion point for the mail would serve you much better. Much like the commissary building. Hell, that even has some empty rooms, secure them properly and use that. Another thought comes to mind. I thought mail was a federal job. Maybe the United States postal Service owes me for eight years of passing out their mail, and then again maybe not.

The "open concept visiting room" was another of my pet peeves. Yes, you heard it right, "open concept" in a maximum-security prison. The inmates not only had personal contact with friends and family, they routinely received sexual favors, literally in front of guards and other visitors! It didn't matter if there were children or elderly watching. The one way the mail and the visiting room were connected was this; When passing out mail on a daily basis, I would observe inmates receiving payment vouchers with the exact odd amount written on it and going to the same female person outside the institution. Payment vouchers were like receipts of authorization for monies that were dispersed from an inmates account. For example: I would see say several vouchers go to several different inmates with the amount of say $40.12 and made out to the same woman. More often then not, the same exact inmates that had received these vouchers had visits during that week. Doesn't take a brain surgeon to figure out what was happening here.

Not to mention the fact that many times the visiting room might have an unruly inmate or a fight. On many occasions visitors were sprayed with gas and or hurt because they were not physically separated from the inmates during the visits. This is way past gross negligence on the part of the administrations... this goes way beyond laxity folks. Their defense on this matter might go something like this: this is a standard visiting room environment that many maximum prisons use today. Well in rebuttal I only have the comment do it right, and not necessarily like other prisons. As I could also say that many maximum-security prisons also use close concept visiting rooms!

I guess I can't blame the Department of Corrections for not attacking the many problems years before. I mean shit, there were so many problems and at so many different levels, they must of felt quite overwhelmed to say the least. I had many discussions with the sergeant in B-East and we became good friends. He always said the same thing when I would complain about the way the prison ran. He would say, "Thomas, this prison has always been fucked up, it's fucked up now, and it will always be fucked up! No matter what you and I do, it will always remain that way. So don't stress, we will both come and go and this prison will remain fucked up as always." At least that was the gist of it anyway. Keep in mind also; these conversations were way before I would realize his argument had some validity.

I still am an optimist to a certain extent and I believe things can change for the better, but my god where do you start?

Back before I went off the deep end, I really disagreed with his theories and felt change could be made one person at a time, but Stateville wore me down, just like it does to many who pass through it's liquidizer like atmosphere.

Sergeant Bigosh had is own views when it came to the administration. He had been there approximately ten years and had seen and experienced a lot of bullshit from both sides. A good example of his realistic philosophy came one day on the usual 3-11 shift and during a third recount. Recounts were plentiful, as I had stated before, due to the doors being inoperable. The administration didn't mind one recount or maybe two, but the third brought more factors into play, such as having to contact Springfield. By the time a third count would be ordered, the potentiality of an escape became more of a worry, and the administration of course became increasingly uncomfortable.

Well on this night, I was assigned the bottom two galleries, two and four. I had counted my galleries several different times, not to mention the rest of the cell house with the other officers several times. It was fast approaching 8:30pm and this count was supposed to have checked around 4:30pm. As a matter of fact, we were supposed to have gone into count procedures again for the second count at 9:30pm.

The inmates needless to say hadn't been fed due to the miss-counts and the warden had just arrived in the institution to chew some ass! The sergeant was completely satisfied with the count in our cell house and as such, sent the officers to chow, four hours later than normal. When I left to go to chow everything seemed quite. As I was returning from chow with the other officers I walked back into the unit with the warden, who was eyeballing the joint. The first thing we observed was about a dozen or so inmates out on the flag. This really enraged him. He started screaming, "Who is assigned this gallery?" "Who is assigned this damn gallery?" My loving sergeant said calmly "why Thomas is assigned two and four sir". So the warden starts screaming at me asking why these inmates are out and lock them back up etc...etc. I pretty much emphatically stated the doors were inoperable and he had just witnessed me re-entering the unit right along with him, which means I hadn't let them out. So he acts as though he doesn't have a clue about the doors, and says "Officer we are on a third re-count get these convicts re-secured!" I complied of course; knowing full well all he was doing was grand standing.

He of course knew the fact the doors were able to be kicked open, but he also felt the need to dump on someone now, because the problem was reflecting back on him...hmmm kind of appropriate don't you think?

Well the warden leaves the unit and we do get a count check a while later, but by this time; I'm extremely pissed off. I hadn't deserved his shit, and besides, this was a great time to make a needed point! I decided I would write each and every inmate that was out of his cell a disciplinary report. Not that I felt it would do any good mind you, but because I needed to blow off some steam and strike back a bit.

Sergeant Bigosh goes on to explain that my writing the tickets is a complete waste of time and that I had other things to do. I was pissed at him to for getting a kick out of the warden chewing on me, and I knew writing the tickets was my call, so I continued. I wrote like a dozen or so. While I was writing, I decided I had another option that according to Sergeant Bigosh was also a waste of time. I would write out a 434 explaining the problems of the doors and write a work order for each door that was out of order. This too, I felt would get back at the him a bit and defiantly get some badly needed attention, while all the time staying in the boarders of my job description. I was loving this way to much to begin to convey to you, since I felt I was striking back at the powers for all the wrongs I felt had been done to me, while they sat idly by.

Sergeant Bigosh observes this tower of papers and reports and says "Thomas, you really don't want to turn in all that paperwork, I know this administration and they will not get a kick out of your sarcastic attempt at humor". I replied it was my job, and they should consider themselves lucky, I didn't write work orders on half the doors in the unit! I knew of course it would take too long to write reports on each and every door, so I made copies of everything and dispersed them to the warden, the warden of operations and even the warden of programs, so they couldn't say they hadn't received them. Looking back, writing all the paperwork was probably a good way of covering myself considering everything, but I was more concerned at that point with the badly needed retaliation and humor factors that were involved.

Well, when I came back the next day for the 3-11 shift, Sergeant Bigosh's suspicions were validated. Just as we walked into the unit from roll call, the phone rings and the sarge' says, Thomas you know who this is don't you? As he picks up the phone, he listens a quick second and motions to me that he is right, and its one of the wardens on the other end. Well he says the warden of operations Warden Shoegig wants to see me right away. Well considering the beginning of the shift is as busy as any other part or more so, I figure he is pretty pissed off.

When I arrive, I see the usual, a big office, big desk, pictures and certificates from god knows where, and the Master of Ceremonies sitting behind his desk leaning back. He is sitting behind this mountain of paperwork, which appeared to be all three copies of everything I had completed the day before. He calmly inquires as to what the hell I thought I was trying to accomplish. I calmly retort, "with all due respect, they're tickets and work orders sir". Then he asked me straight up "if I was jumping on a bandwagon created by another officer" that was also tired of the shit. Mr. Operations was of course referring to another employee that had made public some of the improprieties of this wonderful institution. I said, "No sir," I felt

I was doing my job in advising them of the inoperable doors since the warden seemed to be totally in the dark as to my accusations the day before. Of course you and I know better! Besides I love sarcasm. He advised me that the reports would "HAVE TO STAY IN THE FILES! Of course I knew what he meant. He was simply putting it to me nicely. I was screwed from this point on in regards to promotions or anything else he might have a hand in. The other officer only wanted that damn light bulb changed in a room where deadly weapons were loaded and unloaded. She got rather perturbed when after several weeks the bulb wasn't replaced. I have to admit, I see her point. I do realize the doors are a completely different concern, but the point being here, is she couldn't even get a bulb changed. That is a totally different work order requiring very minimal effort. Then again isn't there a joke about how many people it takes to screw in a light bulb? Well apparently at Stateville the answer is more than three!! I admired her a lot, because no one stood by her and she ended up transferring to another institution. Maybe if the three stooges had to load shotguns in the dark they would have acted a bit more promptly.

Cameras were another laugh. When I first started they didn't even have them in the units. As they arrived in B-East, I welcomed them with open arms. This created a new problem. Some of the lieutenants found it more satisfying to go to the main control center and watch the units run from there. This of course, was where the feeds from the different cameras went to. So if anything did jump, the lieutenant would have to run all the way back to the unit to assist. It was only a minute away, but if you're the one in the shit, those moments were crucial.

Either way the cameras didn't last long, due to the inmates destroying them by fire or whatever. And once destroyed, they remained as a reminder of the impotence of the administration. They did last a bit longer than B-West though, so I guess I should count my blessings.

Back to the visiting room for a brief moment. Once the inmates were done with their visits, they were to be shaken down for contraband. This tied up at least one officer and sometimes two or three, depending on the visitor list. Note to future administrations: if you don't use an open concept visiting room, you can save money by not having to shake down the inmates every day.

What was funny was the shakedown room was interlock style as well, with a door coming in from the visiting room and one leading out back into the tunnels. The shakedown area itself located in-between those doors. For the first five or so years I was at Stateville these doors couldn't even be locked. Except of course unless you count the little sliding lock that looked as though it should have been used on an outhouse door somewhere. And then even that was only on one of the doors not both of them. What an extremely dangerous joke this place actually was.

This same visiting room was the site of many incidents that could, and should have been avoided all together. I remember one instance in particular where a new employee had his jaw broken trying to do his job the way he was taught, but finding out rather decisively what they teach isn't exactly what works. The officer was trying to confiscate some contraband from a high-ranking gang member. He was new and didn't have a clue what the real deal was. Since this was a high-level gang member, it took literally seconds for his counterparts to get wind he was being harassed by the officer, and as such received some on-the-job real-time training. By the time other officers arrived his jaw had been broken. It took this literal unpleasant incident to have the locks on the doors put into place. When all along they should have been there. Open concept visiting room and NO locks...duh! I really don't have to drop a note to the future administrations here do I?

Another game the inmates played, and played well mind you was the "shoe switch". The inmates would wear a pair of state issued shoes into the visiting room. Then when no one was looking, (and sometimes they were actually looking) they would quickly exchange those for an expensive pair of outside street sneakers such as Air Jordan's. The miserably funny thing here is, when the brass would notice an inmate with shoes not state issued, they expected front line staff to retrieve them! Since these shoes where a status symbol and since usually the individual wearing them were of the upper crust of inmates, this wasn't an easy task. And sometimes officers got hurt attempting to retrieve shoes that were there due to the negligence of the same clowns that ordered the retrieval!

The next example had to do with the mail and the visiting room together. On a daily basis I would deliver payment vouchers to the inmates. These little gems allowed the inmates to pay outside sources cash from their individual accounts. What I would notice was that I would be giving these payment vouchers to several different inmates, but they would have the same person (female) as the recipient of the cash. The other weird thing was the amount would be for an odd amount (attempting to draw little attention I guess). Say $42.02. What these inmates where actually doing was meeting this same woman in the visiting room for an unscheduled unauthorized sexual liaison. In some ways it looked as though the inmates were very clever, but on the other hand watching the so-called administration appearing to do their respective jobs, I would change the word "clever" to "opportunistic".

Whenever the concept of contraband would be brought up in conversations with the wardens they usually responded with "the majority of the problem is staff". That very well could be, but another of my favorite laughers comes to mind here.

Mr. Operations comes to roll call one day carrying a large poster board. Maybe he felt like he needed to use those markers in his desk. On the poster board is a long list of contraband seized on a recent prison wide shakedown. On it is everything from cellular phones, to a small washer and VCR. He is insinuating the staff brought it in, and I of course hold up my hand and admit freely, I snuck the washer in my underwear. (Only kidding)

Funny thing is, wardens are not subject to being shook down either in person or their respective vehicles!

Up until the last year I was there, officers were not even shook down properly. Sometimes as an officer you were shook down and sometimes you weren't. Sometimes they just gave you the "Hey how you doing" pat down. Of course if your were a dirty officer, you could wait till just a couple minutes before roll call to finally show up for work and they just rushed you through so you could make it to roll call! What a farce. Note for future administrations: make the shake down room PART of the daily grind, just like roll call. Not an option.

I know, might have to spend more money... can't do that! The hell with security, if something happens we'll just blame it on staff...yes that's it.

Ok, enough about the contraband and the visiting room for a bit. Lets talk about the wonderful world of segregation. Segregation you see is the place where real bad inmates go when they act up in normal institutional situations. Actually and in reality, the inmates look at segregation as a break from the rat race. They still have television and radios, and food delivered to their door. It wasn't really punishment; only thing they didn't have was the option of running around the prison. They still had yard and phone privileges and since the segregation unit has cell house help, anything the inmates needed on the illegal side could be received as a favor or purchased. I did feel for the officers assigned segregation though because some inmates could slip their cuffs off when being transported to the hospital, visits or whatever.

This also brings to mind two incidents. Some new recruits had come to the prison to get a little "on the job", if ya' know what I mean. Well little did they know they would receive plenty of that. The brass had the bright idea to take them to segregation and use the extra bodies for a segregation wide shakedown. Seems like a good idea at first glance, but several new recruits got involved in a melee because too many inmates were out of their cells at once, and some slipped their "not so properly put on cuffs", (Note to future administrations and lieutenants of segregation, cuff from the back always, or better yet; cuff the inmates to the wall of the gallery with those little do-hickeys the police have installed on their walls) and even a couple so called trusted cell house help got involved.

Ok again, I know what you're thinking; this isn't the fault of the administration, right? Actually it is, because if things were done correct on a daily basis those new recruits wouldn't need to have been there in the first place! ON the cell house help... NOT in segregation boys! Rent a clue. Oh yes, that's a note to future administrations as well. Guess notes to the future administrations should have their own chapter, but I like the humor of putting them along side the tribulations at issue.

On another occasion I was escorting an inmate to the hospital for some tests, and an officer from segregation had cuffed him before I arrived. As we are walking along I look up and he is pulling a cigarette out of his mouth. As I look a little closer he is lighting it. I can't believe my eyes, one hand is in cuffs connected to his belt and the other is free. I ended up re-securing the hand of course and he didn't intend any harm to me, but what a trip!

Since we are laughing here, lets continue with another of the Department of Corrections bright ideas, "The Jaycee Program". I mean hey, the inmates didn't have enough already to do, so lets give them another vehicle to actively fuck the state and the employees along with it.

The inmate's were literally affiliated with The Jaycees (No disrespect intended for this worth while organization). This really ridiculous scenario involved certain inmates...(and again usually upper echelon types) running little stores known as Jaycee shacks. The inmates had one shack in each unit and one in the main yard. Inmates were allowed to purchase "Jaycee coupons" which acted as money and of course were another avenue for extortion. With these little coupons they could purchase pop, pizza and other items. Now instead of cigarettes being the main legal tender in the prison, the Jaycee coupons were the preferred method of compensation. I know; the administration is going to argue that these coupons had the name of the inmates who were supposed to use them written clearly on them, so that inmate HAD to use them. OK...real ...slow... for the bright ones out there... Inmates were the ones collecting the vouchers, so do you think they gave a rat's ass if they accepted them from the wrong person? I don't think so. Note for future administrations: NO Jaycee shacks at maximum joints. The other problem with the Jaycee program was that it was used for get-togethers on the yard. This was nothing more than another excuse for gang get-togethers on the south yard. All under the smoke screen of Jaycee sponsored picnics.

If I were to argue about decisions made by the boys at the top, it would be this in a nutshell. Give privileges to the inmates in direct proportion to their security status. IE: If you are going to utilize something as ridiculous as a Jaycee shack in the prison curriculum, do it at the minimum joints and sparingly at the mediums.

Going back to Warden Curly, I believe he was the genius who initiated the Jaycee shack concept in the first place. Since he originated from the juvenile end of the correctional spectrum, I do believe that he felt the inmates were like his kids to a certain respect. You would think if he knew some of them and yes, he knew quite a few, that seeing them again would have made him realize that they fucked up again somewhere down the line or they wouldn't be meeting again. I don't believe Curly saw it that way, and so we ended up with the Jaycee Shacks, not to mention a few other programs that he felt would curb the kids need for violence. We of course, the officers, the chosen few, were able to reap the benefits of his philosophy. Usually in a negative manner though! Well, I have rambled enough for now, let's head back to B-East for some more cell house escapades.

As I began to get a grip on the workings of the cell house, I tried to learn who was running each gang and I do believe I became very proficient at that endeavor. There was a specific hierarchy in each gang and it was a trick keeping up with the ever-changing regimes. The inmates were constantly maneuvering amongst themselves for power so this wasn't always the easiest of tasks.

You always had to be mentally updating your knowledge of the different gangs and their individual hierarchy's. Quite often an officer that was new or an officer from outside the population would come in to replace an officer who had a day off, or called in sick. When we would began to discuss who was who as far as the gangs were concerned, the general reaction was why does it make a difference to me, they're all convicted felons regardless. Since these temporary officers wouldn't be in the population for any lengthy period of time they refused to believe having knowledge of the different gangs was of any importance what's so ever. The hardcore every day "pop" officer knew different. Knowing the gangs was synonymous with knowing the environment. As an officer assigned a cell house you had to exist, and with that in mind, you had better know the environment.

I remember a new officer who came to B-East. He had been a professional wrestler or so he said. He had a washboard stomach and forearms the size of my thighs. I mean the whole nine yards. He had no problem taking off his shirt to show off his physique either. This guy looked like he couldn't be intimidated by anyone. Nonetheless, a short time after he started, he resigned. The cell house banter was that he had been confronted by one of the gangs because he had the superman mentality and he decided it just wasn't worth his effort, so he resigned.

The cell house was actually a little twilight zone. So if you were insane or on your way, it was kind of like an amusement park roller coaster ride whose tracks changed on a nightly basis. If you were one of the tough guys, you could attempt to hide behind your badge and get your jollies that way. Of course that was a game I most certainly didn't recommend. Besides having that badge to begin with meant you were a pawn already, and that was game enough.

The tough guy syndrome can be summed up with this example alone. I had been at Stateville about a year and a half or so when an officer was murdered because he thought he was doing his job and the gangs felt differently. He was a keen observer and had a good sense of where the gangs where holding their stash. Right before he was murdered, a letter listing potential targets of the inmates found it's way into the shift commander's office, it had been signed by "THE EXECUTIONER". It was in fact a list of probable assault victims.

When I first got wind of this letter, I too felt it was just inmates playing mind games with the administration and staff. The administration also felt the same way, and ignored the letter. This officer, who I will not give a nickname to out of respect, lost his life because the administration didn't take the letter seriously. The letter appeared to be in order of importance, in reference to officers or brass that had fucked with the gangs one too many times. I do also realize that hindsight is 20/20 as they say, but they could have put people on the list at different posts till they received a bit more information.

If those on the list were obvious targets for retaliation of some sort, they definitely should have been given different assignments. Who else would know better if the list had some validity then the administration? This particular officer's name should have rang a bell, because he had found several large caches of drugs and contraband and was known to almost flaunt his apparent sixth sense amongst officers and inmates alike.

I do also acknowledge the fact that the wardens can't panic every time a crackpot decides to write a letter, but would you say the following scenario warrants itself to close scrutiny? The day this officer was executed, he was running a line of inmates by himself (there was always supposed to be two officers running a line). Why was he alone? He was also running this line through an area where the towers and or cameras were far and few between. On this particular day a whiteshirt was conspicuously absent from a post that was only yards from the execution point! Last but not least, why were inmates able to spring on him with pipes and beat him to death while going totally undetected throughout the whole assault? No commotion, no nothing. Well the good news is the perpetrators did eventually get caught; the bad news is they received a life sentence. So much for the state taking care of it's own!

They did pass a law making it a felony to assault an officer shortly after that. Little help it did the deceased. Executing those cocksuckers wasn't a choice... it was mandatory!

I pray for the officers I left behind, and I thank the lord everyday that I was able to survive while in that clusterfuck they call a prison. Shouldn't have assaulting an officer been a felony all along, and who was the brains behind the old law? I mean it was actually a misdemeanor to assault an officer!

Which brings to mind another law that changed while I was at Stateville. There was a time when if by chance, an inmate was caught with a shank, the officer was supposed to write a ticket and the inmate would go in front of the inmate review board. If he was found guilty and that was a big if, he received an extended stay at Hotel Segregation. They finally revised this situation and when an inmate was found to be in possession of a shank, the inmate went to court and more time was added to his sentence. I realize that changing the laws is required to achieve the best for all concerned, but aren't some of these changes common sense to begin with? Its even possible I guess that the law was on the books all along, but they sure didn't seem to utilize it much.

The most intense memory for me about that officer, who gave his life for a system that didn't give a shit, was the actual day he was murdered. I was in roll call listening to the usual pep talk. Usually there were three or four whiteshirts present at roll call with their collective radios going crazy (this was of course due to, to little airspace for so many transmissions). I hear they have since purchased new radios...whoopee!! I say purchase new administrators! Well anyway, as they began to turn the radios down so the shift captain could hand out the assignments for the day, I hear the transmission that all K3* units 10-25 Unit G. I dismissed this as the usual radio banter, because in roll call an officer would here all kinds of bullshit coming over the radio while some was valid, and some not.

Roll call ended and as we proceeded to our respective assignments, we were in the process of passing gate five, and I saw several officers running toward me either running by or pushing what appeared to be an inmate on a gurney completely covered in blood. I had dark sunglasses on at the time and as they passed, another officer made the comment that it was an officer on the gurney.

The body was so saturated with blood I couldn't tell that it was an officer. Our uniforms were green and the blood made the uniform appear blue. Blue was the color of the inmates clothing, at least when they were wearing state issue anyway. My heart goes out to the family of that officer. Not because he is the only officer to ever die, but his death could have been avoided and the real deal behind his death might never come to light.

On a different note, my humor has changed a lot since working for the department. A story that I laugh at now that I probably wouldn't have fifteen years ago goes something like this. There were a few inmates I actually got along with. Some because the conversation was good and some who just didn't make it their daily endeavor to fuck with me. This one inmate with the appropriate cell house name of Romeo, never gave me a lick of heartache. As a matter of fact I felt I could have had a beer with him if he and I were to have met on the streets. One day when I was locking up four gallery I found out the story behind his incarceration.

The story goes that he had a falling out with his significant other. Either she had an affair or whatever; but it must have been a major issue, or at least to him anyway. It seems she pissed him off to the point that he killed her, then decapitated her. I realize that's not very funny, but I felt the second part of the story was. After cutting of the head, I guess he walked into a bar holding the head by the hair, and then proceeded to sit the head on the bar and gave a pointing gesture to the head with his thumb as a hitchhiker would do, and said to the bartender "I think she NEEDS a drink!!!! He apparently sat there and sipped his drink until the police arrived. Now I know, to the majority of people that's pretty sick, but I find it humorous to this day, sorry. I don't know for sure if this story is in fact true but I still found it amusing.

Immediately after the officer mentioned a few minutes ago died, the institution went on lockdown. We remained on lockdown for pretty much an entire summer, accounting for the longest lockdown while I was employed at the penitentiary. It was in the heart of the summer, and we fed the inmates at their cells and delivered restricted commissary to them. They started fires and we put them out; they threw food and we cleaned it up. That summer was a summer of sweeping and sweating. Thank god there was this exceptionally cold, water fountain in the cell house. To bad the water wasn't healthy! Along with many other officers I drank gallons of the stuff. I didn't know this at the time of course, but I would find after a lawsuit brought on by the inmates that the EPA had tested the water and found it to contain excessive levels of lead, radium, microscopic worms and several other carcinogens. I drank from this fountain for at least two years I know of. Heck, on many occasions a white powdery substance fell on officer's shoulders in the sergeant's office. I would learn later I had been exposed repeatedly to asbestos! During lockdown that summer our day went something like this:

We would enter the unit and began our count. Since the inmates for the most part were secured already the count usually checked rather quick. We passed out the mail and an officer or two went to chow. The officers that remained cleaned the excess garbage left from the day shift. Believe me on those hot days that garbage gave a new meaning to the word rancid. Then after those all-important logbooks and forms were filled out we fed the little angels their evening meal. We then waited eagerly twenty to thirty minutes while they threw the garbage on to the galleries and onto the flag. Then we would proceed to sweep and mop the entire unit. Continually dodging projectiles thrown from the upper galleries. Eventually it was time for the 9:30pm count. Somewhere along this line, the administration felt the poor babies were getting entirely too hot in their cells and decided we should pass out ice twice each day. The job itself took the better part of an hour. The ice that we passed out to each inmate, lasted about ten minutes tops. I am not saying they should stay in the cell and roast, but damn we were humping the ice in used garbage cans lined with a fresh garbage bag!

After roughly a month on lockdown, the mixture of food and heat produced a stench that only a correctional officer can relate to. The inmates were beginning to get a touch anxious themselves and began to set more fires and through apples, pears or bars of soap through the windows on the opposite wall. Since my patience was wearing a bit thin as well, I had no problem getting on the intercom and advising the inmates that the same windows they were busting, to obtain a better breeze and piss off the officers, would be the same windows that would eventually allow old man winter an entrance. Sure enough this time, the inmates paid for the administrations lack of attentiveness. Winter did arrive and damn it was cold! I even felt a bit sorry for the new inmates that had arrived and had nothing to do with the lockdown or the vandalism in the first place.

Well we would ultimately make it through the lockdown and that hot summer; but my favorite memory of the time was when we were feeding the usual bullshit supper one evening. Every meal usually contained one fresh fruit of some sort. For this particular meal though, we were delivered four hundred cantaloupes to hand out. We were supposed to hand out one to each inmate in the unit. It might sound like a good idea considering the weather as it was, but we were on lockdown. The hole in each of the cell doors that we utilized to feed was not large enough for the fruit to go through. All the same, I was required to pass out one to each inmate. Well I walked down the galleries along with the other officers and we literally stuffed the fruit into the bars just enough to hold it there. After I completed passing out the fruit, I looked down the gallery and there were fifty-eight cells trying to figure out how to get the cantaloupe in to the cells. I left and came back about fifteen minutes later and just like magic all the fruit had found it's way into each and every cell. The ones that couldn't just open there cell doors and get the fruit from the bars, had utilized shanks to cut the fruit in half and slip it through the opening in the cell door.

Let me tell you a little about the preferred weapon of the incarcerated; the shank. I saw everything from crude bent metal, to shanks that looked as though they had been purchased at a sporting goods store, and everything in between. As I said at the beginning, there were grinders in different areas of the industry buildings. Note to future administrations: No grinders! They also used large rocks to accomplish the sharpening, but maybe if they didn't have the grinders some of those shanks wouldn't have resembled a razor sharp cutlass. They even designed sheaths for some of the shanks.

They had some interesting ways of hiding the shanks as well. Sometimes they put them in the hollow bars of the bed frames. Other times an officer could find them in the sink connected to the wall. The metal sinks were hollow and it had a little thingamajig on the side that was for hanging a washcloth or small towel. The inmates would take off the little thingamajig and slip the shanks in to the hollow sink, and then replacing the thingamajig so the sink looked normal. Each shank had a loop on the end made of string or whatever and they could be fished out of the hole as needed. Sometimes they connected all the shanks so they could get them all quickly.

An officer could easily tap the underside of the sink with his open palm and determine if shanks were there, but with the continual turnover of officers this hiding spot probably still works to this day. The inmates also took apart the fluorescent light fixtures, placed the shanks in the opening and put the fixture back in place. This was a good spot because sometimes shakedowns had to be quick because of time restraints and this spot was not checked. If the cell door itself had enough play, which was most of the time, the inmates could hide them there as well. My favorite spot of all though, had to have been when they hid them right next to the wall. First, they placed the shanks on the floor right next to the wall. Second, they would melt bars of soap and cover the shank or shanks. Third, they would freshly paint their cells and wham, to the naked eye...no shanks! If the inmate was good at forming the soap and had a little talent at painting, the shank was literally invisible, but yet he had very quick, easy access. Who said these convicts aren't creative?

Since we are on the subject of weapons, lets dabble in the second favorite weapon of the unjustly accused, the pipe. Hell, Mr. Green used it in the study hundreds of times, why not inmates in a maximum-security facility?

When I initially started in B-East, there was so much neglect regarding maintenance to the cell house, that pipes were readily available almost anywhere you looked. They have since resolved this problem to a certain extent, but back then, most of the bars on the outside of the galleries were either missing already or well on there way. It took very little effort over time to bend a piece of bar from the gallery till it broke away; almost to the point where the inmate could decide on this size of the weapon. The bars at that time served no purpose other than to provide the inmates with a continual fresh supply of weapons. The longer I stayed in B-East the more the bars continued to vanish. Yes, of course we made out work orders…I hope I don't have to explain that concept again!

The admin finally replaced the worn out bars (the ones that were left anyway) with more modern sectional bars that seemed to suit the galleries a little better. These too had a minor flaw as they decreased the line of sight from the catwalk. I was thankful for the change regardless. They also decided to put gates on the ends of each gallery, which totally enclosed each gallery. NO more spiders, and no more climbing up and down from one gallery to another. Wow, score one for the brass! Well almost…the gates on the end of the galleries used padlocks that were a bitch to unlock if you were coming from the opposite side. Not only were they stupid enough not to design the door so the lock could be accessed from either side easily, they actually should have designed the doors to use the heavy Folger-Adams locks that required the large prison type keys. Oh well, I give them gold stars for their half ass attempt anyway. If your were leaving the gallery you had to reach through the door and undue the padlock. If there was an emergency, god I hope you had acquired some practice! This of course was just another example of fixing something, but not fixing it right. Even if you were not in a rush, you still had to turn your back to inmates that might happen to be on the gallery a lot longer than if Folger-Adam type locks were utilized.

This brings to mind one of those ridiculous sheets we had to fill out every day. The bar rap sheet. We were expected to log on this sheet everyday and sign same, that we had checked each and every bar for damage. This was before the new bars mind you! We were expected to rap bars that were close to non-existant, or bars on doors that could be kicked open! What a continual joke this place really was.

On the protection side, we had the comfort of the catwalks with their eight round allotments. Let me see, In B-East and B-West there were four hundred inmates and eight rounds...F-House on the other hand was the round house, which housed approximately two hundred and sixty inmates. Its tower located in the middle with direct view of the entire unit not only had twenty rounds of #00 buckshot but in addition forty rounds of Mini-14 ammunition.

The administration will scream that F-House inmates are classified as more volatile, and to a certain extent that isn't a bad argument, but when everything is added and subtracted, it just doesn't make sense. We did of course have those canisters mounted on the wall that were rumored to contain gas. I remember the officers talking one day; pondering if they really did have canisters inside or if they worked at all. The dust on them was as thick as moss. One day some maintenance men came in and serviced them. They had to cut holes in the chain link fence surrounding the catwalk to access and service the canisters properly. I realize the inmates could have accessed the catwalk from the fire escape anyway, but they left the holes after servicing the gas canisters, giving the inmates yet another option.

I really think that the majority of the officers liked the job even with all the neglect and danger around each corner. It just seemed that everywhere you looked, you were met with neglect of some sort. The gates in the tunnels were another example. These were used to attempt to control movement and divide the tunnel in case of a major insurrection. The gates for the longest time were easily pushed open. The gates were driven by a motor chain mechanism that obviously didn't exert enough pressure.

Lets talk about the inmate's commissary choices for a bit. Upon my departure from Stateville, the commissary list was twenty plus pages long printed on both sides. Don't get me wrong here; I believe inmates should be allowed a certain amount of items of which to choose. It's just that security level proportion thing again. Those type of options belong in the minimum joints not the max joints. Examples... ok...the list comprised about 425 items. There were items on the list that caused the death of a Captain who later died and was only two weeks from retirement (But more on that later). The inmates at that time had six watch styles to choose from, three television models, four radio styles and a host of other items. My favorite item though, without a doubt, was the SPF 40 Sunblock. Then again, if I were in prison I would want to look young and vibrant too! Or perhaps pretend I was at the beach and mentally escape for an afternoon.

The inmates had an option called "Special Trades". This was a trump card they could play whenever the tickets some poor officer had written were actually starting to hurt a bit. Special trades had no hard or steadfast rules, except they could be approved by a superintendent or a warden and allowed for the inmate to circumvent what little power the officer actually had. I don't know how many times an inmate would walk by me with a sack of commissary flaunting the fact he had it, regardless of my tickets. Some were even brazen enough to make a snide remark as well. Sure, sometimes I wrote a ticket on their tidbit of verbal diarrhea, but what was the point really. Then again, I still had stock in the Bic pen company!

The longer I remained in B-east, the more intently the imaginary monkeys clung to my back. As I reflect, my enthusiasm for the job went from ten to zero. The place was so fucked up, that even my initial enthusiasm had worked its way to literal disgust for the whole system. I began to drink every single night after work and no matter how hard I tried, I couldn't leave the damn job at the prison, like I was told to do from day one. I brought the futility of the environment home with me almost nightly.

The inmates were constantly filing frivolous lawsuits for one reason or another. This started to bother me; I started thinking about the rights of inmates and the rights of the officers. This made it literally impossible for me to even go to work, not to mention, function in a professional manner if I did go. Some of the lawsuits had merit of course, but there were such a large percentages that were such a farce.

Back in the days of Alcatraz, the pendulum of inmate's rights was to the extreme left. Even with all my dreadful recollections, I don't advocate extreme measures such as those either! Those extremes were definitely wrong. At the time, the outcry was for inmates rights and justifiably so. They are not animals and shouldn't be treated as such, but then again they shouldn't have the plethora of rights and choices they do today! Primarily those inmates incarcerated in maximum-security facilities.

The majority of inmates in the system today come from the most run down, drug infested areas in the state. So the thought of a roof and three meals a day along with medical care that they probably didn't have before, along with activities up the ying-yang doesn't really pose a serious threat to there already meager existence.

There should be distinct proportional differences between the different level institutions. So an inmate doesn't savor the thought of being housed in a max joint. If he is unfortunate enough to be already be housed at maximum-security institution, it should be that he was fucked from the front door and can't wait to get re-classified so he can go to a medium and on to a minimum. The benefits in the prisons should increase as the security level decreases. I really do apologize for being redundant on this matter, but someone really... really needs to listen. I know what your thinking, what about the guy doing two life terms or four hundred years? What do they have to strive for?

I will put it to ya this way; don't do the crime, if ya can't do the time. Fuck those dudes; they didn't receive those extended sentences because they were nice. Maybe if the State actually gave inmates something to strive for they could actually and effectively use terms like "life behavior modification" in the proper context. OK, here is a simple example, listen up…at the minimum joints you can be disciplined for literally walking on the grass instead of the sidewalk. Try switching this around to the maximum penitentiaries. NO REALLY! You make it so the benefits are literally non-existent at the maximum level, where they literally can't do shit, and proportionately augment the inmates benefits as the security level goes down.

One thing the administration did teach me was to cover my ass well. They sure as hell weren't going to, and if they had half a chance, and it meant saving their collective rear ends, they would nail your sorry ass quicker then shit!

One incident that had me close to that state of affairs rings well. I was acting sergeant in B-East, and the chow line was returning normally. Everything appeared ordinary as usual, and I am pretty sure I was telling the officers how all seemed well in Stateville land. More than likely I failed to knock on wood immediately after that comment because the phone rang. It was the shift commander Captain Kuffingston. He told me to report to the infirmary as quickly as I could get there.

The urgency in his voice had me totally confused to say the least. Not only that, it was getting late in the shift when things get really busy, and he still wanted me to leave the unit. When I arrived at the infirmary Captain Kuffingston asked me to identify the inmate laying on the gurney that the medical personnel were working on. As I was moving closer I wondered for a second why he asked me to identify the inmate. Just as quickly as the indecision of who he was captured my thoughts, the realization of who he actually was really astonished me.

It was J.W. the Mickey Cobra chief for B-East. As I relayed this information to the captain, knowing pretty much then that he already had an idea, he quickly responded with "tell me why he was found in the B-West shower? He then went on to explain, "He was stabbed in the B-West shower and was dieing right in front of me". I told him "I didn't have a clue why he was in the B-West shower except that our chow line had went out about a half an hour prior." He told me to do my paperwork and get back with him as soon as humanly possible. I could feel the administrational vice squeezing as each second ticked by. I knew they would look for a sacrifice if the inmate were to die. There would be no way they took the heat in any way, shape or form.

There was blood all over J.W. and the medical personnel were attempting to restart his heart. He did in fact end up dying, and it centered on the story that an inmate from B-West wanted to take his spot, on the top of the heap for the MCs in B-East. J.W. entered B-West with their chow line and apparently assumed that he was meeting some guy in the shower to smoke a joint or discuss something totally unrelated to the actual agenda. Obviously the wrong guy showed up and tried to force a change in power and J.W wouldn't go for it. J.W was murdered and that's when I came into the picture.

The responsibility appeared to have fallen completely on the B-West door officer, even though the door officer wrote a report stating the B-West sergeant authorized J.W.'s entrance into the unit. Even if the officer had asked for authorization, inmates move around so quickly that determining who is who is impossible when a chow line returns. Back then they did have I.Ds but the identification did not list a unit that the inmate was assigned to. Now I understand they do!

The fact of the matter is simply this. The administrations always put their mistakes on the little guy and it takes something major to happen before they even consider changing policy or fixing something. Note for future administrations: Don't be reactive, be proactive. Have the nuts for god's sake to get authorization from Springfield to make changes before it's to late!

Probably my worst memory is when F-House had a riot and the inmates completely took over the unit. Again, on this shift, I just happened to be the acting sergeant in Unit B-East. Captain Kuffingston was going on vacation for a few weeks and this was his last shift. Everything appeared to running like it always had run, when the captain had the bright idea to turn the phones in the institution off a little earlier then the inmates were accustomed to. At least this is was the story that everyone seemed to agree on after the fact. He also wanted to get the institution secure a little earlier, apparently trying to slide into his vacation. Little did he know his actions would result in his having an extended vacation and one I am sure he will always remember.

He did, in fact, turn the phones off early. Several problems occurred here. First, the inmates are accustomed to a set schedule for almost everything they do, day after day, and week after week. Second, not only was the phones being turned off unexpected, but these inmates value phone time just as much as any other commodity, because that's exactly what it is in the joint, a commodity. On each gallery in each cell house there is a phone assigned. The inmates are always making deals concerning phone time and of course the chiefs want their time as well. The inmate phone clerks were always affiliated so they had there own agendas to deal with. So there you have it, the stage was set.

When the phones went off, each unit had similar inquiries by the inmates and the respective sergeants attempted to find out why the phones went off. Understanding of course, that the sergeant is the first of the hierarchy that the inmates can get to, they besieged the different sergeants offices with complaints and questions. I found out by way of main control that this was the order of the night by the shift captain and that was that. I agree that the shift captain should be able to run the place any damn way he wants within reason, but when you have coddled the inmates as long as Stateville had, something had to give, and give it would!

The inmates in my unit were locking up extremely slowly. The were getting progressively agitated, realizing the phones were really off for the night and this wasn't just an outage for a few minutes. I told the officers to be real careful; since I could see even the well-mannered inmates were really pissed off. The catwalk was likewise advised to be very alert and we began our lock up. As each phone clerk came down one by one from his assigned gallery, I had to have pretty much the same conversation over and over, assuring them, I had nothing to do with this, and that all the units had their phones turned off.

As I proceeded down two gallery securing inmates, the inquiries became more deliberate and hostile. They didn't understand what they had done to warrant being locked up earlier then usual and having the phones turned off as well. I told them exactly what I knew, "I told them I didn't know what was going on except it was time to secure and the phones were off and that was that." I could hear over the radio that the other units were having similar problems, with F-House being the most keyed up due to the abundance of heavyweight chiefs housed there.

I noticed that the few inmates that actually did secure, only a few minutes before were actually kicking back out of their cells with or without the assistance of their brothers. At this point, I became extremely concerned. Obviously in the last few minutes the collective attitude of the house had changed considerably or the inmates wouldn't have locked up only a few short minutes prior.

I got on the radio and told the gallery officers to report to the sergeant's office immediately. While in route to the sergeant's office, I figured we could regroup and work together as opposed to individually. For the moment we also would be closer to the unit door. Putting the officers in one group also would afford the catwalk two shotguns in one location covering every officer. As I met the others at the office, I could here over the radio the shift captain was on his way to F-House because the inmates were refusing to lock up. This really didn't alarm me much because I knew the inmates in F-House had used this technique, many times before to get there way. They would all collectively refuse to lock up. Usually the shift captain would go there and play a little diplomacy game and that would be it.

The fact that the officers were working together actually alarmed the inmates and continued inquires were continually being made as to "what were all the changes being made for?" We were starting to make just a little dent in the securing game with the three officers working together, when over the radio my nightmare was being played out. The armory was asking for all available K3 Units to go to F-House. I knew this meant serious trouble, so we went back down to the sergeants office even though more then half the unit was still out, and knowing the half that were secured could easily kick back out.

I decided to call over the telephone to the armory to learn what I could, since the inmates were already hearing enough via the officer's radios. What I found out was that the Shift Captain had been stabbed after going into the middle of F-House flag attempting to bring order. An inmate from one of the Latino gangs had actually jumped on his back and had stabbed him several times. He was supposedly extremely high as well. The tower peppered the inmate with Mini 14 rounds and actually saved the captains life. The tower also though, had inadvertently hit the captain because the captain and the inmate were of course struggling when the officer fired. The captain would survive the attack, but almost died and almost lost an arm.

The inmates in B-East had gotten wind that one of there own had been shot dead in F-House. As the inmates streamed toward the sergeants office, I advised them I was trying to see what was going on so we could get this matter settled. I could see in their eyes they didn't believe a word of my shit. We would confiscate a letter a few weeks later that stated the Latin Disciples were arguing amongst themselves all during that night whether or not to take B-East over.

After I hung up with the armory I realized that any extra staff at all would be tied up in F-House so I decided to take a look outside the sergeant's office to get a feel for what the inmate mood was. Upon walking onto the flag I saw G.S. the leader of the Gangster Disciples coming down the flag towards the sergeants office with about fifty of his soldiers in tow. He had a belt rapped around his hand and a large buckle hanging from the belt. I hesitated just a second before I was going to have the officers hit the unit door, when as if they had another agenda, the entire contingent took a ninety degree turn and walked up the stairs heading towards the upper galleries.

I decided to call the armory again and tell them I thought our unit was in jeopardy. As the phone was ringing I remember I had helped out that old man on the flag before, and he was somewhat under the G.D umbrella, and I also remembered that G.S and I had that conversation about all those tickets I had written on eight gallery and the fact that he at least had said "I would never have another problem out of his people."

The armory finally picked up, obviously very busy and I said, if ya can… quietly get some whiteshirts over here. I told the officers on the catwalk we were going to attempt the lock up one more time. They should not hesitate sprinting to the unit door if something jumped. For some reason though after The Gangster Disciples passed the office I felt we were not in direct danger. They had their chance and for whatever reason didn't take it. I think at that point I was really glad that I was one of the "negotiator types" and that the majority of the unit population felt I was fair. If they had thought any differently, I am sure we would have been in serious trouble. I also believe the many recitations of Psalm 23 didn't hurt our chances either.

Well we proceeded up to the higher galleries to begin again. In the interim I guess, the Latin Disciples decided they had to do something to avenge their dead brother in F-House. They decided to meet at the sergeant's office and deal with whom ever was there at the time. My karma must have been clicking on all cylinders that day, because that's the exact time I locked up the sergeant's office and headed upstairs with the other officers.

I guess as they arrived to see the locked door at the sergeant's office they looked up and saw one of my favorite catwalk officers looking down at them. The inmates knew him as "Crazy", because his eyes bugged out of his head a bit, and his hair was always in a state of disarray. He also played the character up a bit also, by talking shit to the inmates. He was a real nice guy though, but I always played that wild card whenever possible and thank god I did that day. He probably saved my life that day without firing a shot. According to officer Crazy, when they saw the door locked on the sergeant's office and him looking down at them they started arguing. He said he could tell they were divided on what to do next. Half wanted to take retaliatory measures and the other half were arguing that one brother had already died what would be the point. Finally the craziest of the L.D.s retreated to his cell slamming the door of his cell in disgust.

Since we were not accomplishing too much in the realm of securing, we then started to head back down stairs when the unit door opened and a whole shit load of staff were entering the unit. Apparently they had lost F-House and were trying to secure the rest of the institution. We ended up securing the entire unit and we sat in the sergeant's office as the staff left the unit for other endeavors.

One thing did happen though that amazed even me. When we got to the back of the flag to secure the remaining L.Ds, a lieutenant was chewing on a candy bar as we went along. The inmates were less then congenial, but it only took the offer of a candy bar for them to lock up. It really freaked me out. The whiteshirt reached into his pocket and pulled out a candy bar and casually asked the loudest of the group if he wanted it. Then, the inmate takes the candy and quietly goes in his cell. Talk about strange; I mean the last thing I thought that the inmate would do while running his mouth, would be to take that candy bar and go lock-up! We listened on the radio as the officers in F-House tower were hastily requesting to be taken out of the tower.

Inmates were attempting to set the tower on fire by placing mattresses directly under the tower and then lighting them. They also were throwing Molotov cocktails at the tower. As all of this was transpiring, the powers that be, were mobilizing a tactical team generated from all over the state, and they also asked the State Police for assistance in taking the unit back. I understand the inmates were also putting soap on the floors by the entry points of the unit. Another half hour or so had transpired when we found out the entire institution was secure as it could be, all except F-House.

After a couple hours, forces from the combined tactical teams, the state police and our own, entered F-House. They fired several shots into the ceiling to make clear their intentions. Approximately fifteen minutes later the unit was secured. I guess the inmates had been wreaking havoc long enough and had tired a bit.

The following day the spokesman for the Department of Corrections made the statement to the papers that "Stateville was locked up tighter then a drum!"

That following evening I was again back at the Ville' for work, and eating in the officers mess, no pun intended. When a strange transmission came over the radio "They're taking over G-Dorm!" I couldn't believe what I was hearing. Apparently they took the unit in direct retaliation for the prior days events. Several officers were actually taken hostage for a very short period of time. The armory asked that all units send two officers to the armory for re-assignment. I volunteered, but all they did with me was put me on gate five to replace an officer used for armory back up in case of emergencies. So I sat at gate five listening to the radio and watching officers and brass go back and forth.

When they finally took the unit back the entire unit had been trashed, so they put all the inmates on the south yard until they could clean up and re-assign the inmates. One thing kept ringing in my hear "Tighter then a drum"...drum...drum" These people should have taken up comedy for a living, because they had me rolling! If I didn't know the D.O.C. was a joke now I never would.

The shift ended, and as I was leaving I noticed Mr. Operations asking for volunteers to stay and help the cause. There must have been a shred of loyalty left because I stayed as several other officers declined. It was actually kind of interesting. I ended up staying until like eight the following morning. The staff had cleaned up G-Dorm, but several of the rooms were damaged too severally to be used. So some of the inmates were split up between the other units and /or shipped to other penitentiaries.

The night was really interesting though as we watched the inmates on the south yard set fire to pallets used as a standing area for the makeshift showers located there. They screamed crap at us, but for the most part were reasonable considering all that had transpired over the last couple days.

Even though it was summer, the night started to get a bit chilly and the brass decided to move the inmates off the yard and into the law library. The door for the library was about seventy-five yards from the gate of the south yard. As the inmates walked to the library door, there were three shotguns at ground level focused right on the line. The only thing was there was nothing between us, and all those extremely agitated inmates! We did have the south yard tower as well in firing range, and two officers with Mini's manning it.

Even so, it surely was a precarious position to be in. The tactical team was there as well, but were talking about two hundred inmates here. Luckily they went into the library with little difficulty.

Maybe Sergeant Bigosh was right; maybe he and I would come and go and maybe the joint would remain, fucked up for eternity. Continually going through the endless rounds of politics that seemed to encompass it day after day. The problem lies in the fact that these politics were as dangerous as any, and real lives hung in the balance daily. Note for future administrations: Don't negotiate, (isn't this supposed to be a steadfast rule anyway?)

Since I'm all pumped up, I promised earlier I would speak on Captain Dan's behalf. (This is the only name in the book not disguised) he was about two weeks from retirement. He had completed his time in this hellhole. Two weeks before his deserved retirement, inmates beat him with socks filled with batteries. He would later die. WHAT the fuck do inmates at a maximum-security facility need batteries for? Again, I understand if it wasn't batteries it would have been something else, but that's certainly not the point! I figure if ya can't plug it in the wall fuck em'!! This is a max joint re…mem…ber? Captain Dan was killed in the tunnels, were he had been countless times before, his gas canisters lying next to him, so he went out the way you would expect. Just an opinion here and not a note per say, when a seasoned veteran is getting close to retirement, cut his wings if he likes it or not. Send him to the farm, or just put him in a place where these things can't happen. I once again agree that hindsight is 20-20 as I said before but likewise it is simple enough to see what's in front of your face. Captain Dan had no problem pissing off an inmate, and he did little in the way of negotiations. I am sure the concept of him dieing right before retirement was humorous to all the scum he pissed off over the years.

The legislators are part of the problem. Many of the laws they set down do not deal with them directly. One day I decided to go with the Union down to the capital in Springfield. I really didn't know why I was going except to meet some of the clowns that make the laws they don't personally have to enforce. The people I met and had supper with, seemed to me my type exactly. They all were more then ready to battle the Status Quo, and the clowns that were always protecting it.

We spent the day talking with different legislators that were supposedly voting for bills we opposed. Most provided the same political mumbo jumbo that probably earned them their seat to begin with. I tried to be optimistic and go with the flow, but I found myself shaking my head in disgust several times. If we started to make a point, they usually responded with a more firm, "I have my views and that's that" attitude! Hidden agenda's and who was buying the next dinner seemed to be the priorities. Well the day might not have been fun but it was at least enlightening.

Back to The Ville'…Sergeant Bigosh not only gave me endless insight into the workings of the administration, he also inadvertently showed me what the Stateville could do to a personality given enough time.

In the fours years that I worked with him, I watched as his humor became darker, and his sarcasm honed to a fine point. At the end of our four years together he briefly bumped over to G-Dorm and then totally out of Stateville to a more reasonable environment down state. He was a thinker and I hear a master prankster on the midnight shift. He liked to laugh a lot, but all in all I think those were defense mechanisms. Stateville really did suck, and I was learning that finally!

When Sergeant Bigosh would finally leave Stateville after more then fifteen years, he even gave up his sergeant stripes for the transfer, that's how bad he wanted out. I watched as a lot of crews came and went. I watched as a lot of lieutenants, captains and even superintendents came and went. I did liked Lieutenant Tomms a lot because we seemed to click. He was a reliable, fair but firm lieutenant that gave the inmates what they had coming and tried hard to keep the peace.

Lieutenant K. Mistall eventually replaced him. He was also a good supervisor, although brand new. He was an excellent replacement though, because you could count on him for anything and he even went as far as to help sweep on lockdowns. I had never seen that before…quite a shock really; a whiteshirt sweeping…this place never stopped amazing me! I thought that to be very admirable though and I hope he is doing great these days.

He always tried to give the convicts what they had coming, and made it a daily event to help the officers on the galleries. For the most part he never asked an officer to do anything he wouldn't do himself. He didn't just say it, or preach it, he did it!

Well as I said people come and go. Funny thing about fate, when mixed with Stateville karma, you end up with the initial Lieutenant you started with. I couldn't believe this, I mean shit, H-House was rough enough for this guy and now I'm supposed to deal with him in population?

I remember the incident that actually convinced me to get out of B-East for good. I was on six gallery arguing with a rather large, loud mouth. I got on the radio and requested assistance, which I hardly ever did. The illustrious ex-H-house lieutenant was out of the unit, which of course made sense, and by radio he said he would be there shortly to assist me. I stood there playing verbal volleyball with this clown assuming I would have a white shirt on the way. Not much of one, mind you, but a white shirt just the same. So I'm standing there, and I'm standing there. I finally resolved the matter, probably because I bored the inmate to death. This lieutenant who is in a class of his own, never shows up. Several of the inmate's friends were standing around watching as well. I did have the catwalk monitoring the situation, and luckily it didn't escalate, but give me a break!

Then there was Lieutenant G. Tismar. Actually he came before Lieutenant Clusterfuck but I could count on this guy in a different way completely. He showed up any time I called, but negotiator was not one of his attributes and our personalities clashed a time or two. I was perfectly capable of running the unit, but I knew if I called on Tismar, his only reply to a convict's whining would be "Lock Up"!

On one occasion I had an inmate in the bullpen waiting to go to segregation for whatever reason. He was left there from day shift and we were supposed to deal with transportation to segregation. He was highly intoxicated and wanted out of the bullpen real bad. He tried to think of everything he could to get out… He had to piss, he needed a doctor and on it went. Finally he sat down and started to talk to himself, so I started my paperwork for the day. Then he started up again. Usually I would have escorted him to the bathroom but I knew the lieutenant was due any minute and this guy was really wasted. Not to mention the fact that his actions were less then sensible.

I kept explaining to him there would be an escort for him shortly, but he became really agitated and began to urinate on the floor, yelling the whole time "I told ya Mother Fucker, I had to piss!" he actually whipped out his penis and urinated right in front of me.

When the lieutenant walked into the unit he asked what the problem was. I told him, "this guy needed to be escorted to segregation", because he was left over by the day shift. He also was highly intoxicated and pissed on the floor. The lieutenant told me "to be sure to put another ticket on him for the urination incident", and he said, "get the keys, he's out of here". All the while, the inmate was screaming, "I don't give a fuck about another ticket bitch, do what ya' gotta' do!"

The lieutenant ordered him to cuff up, which is the normal procedure. I had a feeling the inmate would refuse, and he confirmed my suspicions. The lieutenant tried to explain to the inmate, from this point on, all bets were off, if he continued to refuse. The inmate continued cursing and making threatening statements. I think the lieutenant was just about to grab his gas when the inmate started yelling, "Send in the little guy!" "Send in the little guy!" Of course he was referring to me, since the lieutenant was upwards of two hundred and thirty pounds. This would be one of those times I was definitely glad to have the lieutenant around. If I had even attempted cuffing this guy alone, I probably would have been the one that ended up in the cuffs. This guy was built rather well, from bottom to top. Well we went in, and began wrestling with this guy, trying not to fall into the urine. We were pretty close, a couple times, but we managed to keep him pinned against the bars of the bullpen and eventually he was escorted to segregation.

On a different note altogether, one thing that was interesting was the way that the inmates communicated with one another. The preferred method of communication when secured was with the use of kites* if of course they weren't lucky enough to be able to get out of their cells or just didn't want to risk getting caught running around. They would put the kites in a laundry bag and connect it to a string made out of yards and yards of torn material. They then were able to get it literally from the top gallery on one side, to the bottom gallery on the other side, all the while locked in their cells. Of course they had the assistance of other inmates in other cells along the way, but no small feat regardless.

The inmates also had cell house names that they either acquired while on the streets or once they had become incarcerated. This could really throw a new officer. I know for a fact, because it did me at the beginning. Unless you knew the inmates more or less personally, and knew the cell house lingo, it was easy to mistake conversations for another language. IE: "Shorty G is getting some kick ass hooch* from Crazy for a brick*." "Nutty Bar might be violated by his cellie* tonight if he doesn't give it up". If I put myself in the right frame of mind while listening to some of this pig Latin I found myself smiling inadvertently.

I made it a point to learn the majority of the inmates cell house names and the language they used. I seemed to make a lot of things a much more clear as I went along. Of course, as I said, there were those employees that could give a rat's ass about whatever the inmates were saying or doing. Some of them actually made this angle work to a certain extent. Maybe having the tough guy demeanor and a bit of luck had something to do with it. I liked my chances a lot better using the knowledge and philosophy angles. Whatever works for you, I guess.

I believe the hard-guy technique worked at one time, many moons ago, but that today's prisons require that you learn the environment as quickly as possible. This includes the language and who is who. The tough-guy angle requires too much luck as a variable to be effective. Prisoners have too many freedoms these days and to many rights to go along with those freedoms. I have seen officers come into the joint with that, "I got THIS attitude" and make it work. More often than not, it doesn't work though. It didn't matter if you were the toughest motherfucker on the planet or just thought you were. The inmates have nothing but time, and they will bide that time and pick the most opportune place. To find out if you not only talk the talk, but walk it as well! Then when your all alone, it will be time to back up your mouth.

Usually the inmates had half a dozen or so buddies and shank or two hidden; just to make sure things went in their favor. Time weighed too heavily against the so-called tuff guys, or at least that's the way I saw it. Inmates as a rule were mostly talk, but when they came at you, they came deep. The amount of inmates that would come at you, was proportionate usually, to how bad the violation* was going to be. Either way, if your number was up, the inmates would find a way to deal with it.

I also understand that the inmates had to appear tough in front of the other residents. On many occasions an inmate would give me the worst time while he was in front of his brothers, and then when he was away from the hustle and bustle it was a totally different story entirely.

What I tried to do was give a little, take a little, in most situations. I noticed that the inmates appreciated it when you went out of your way to be fair to them, even if you were firm and professional at the same time. It didn't matter if you where white, black, male or female. It didn't matter if you were an officer, sergeant, lieutenant or captain. Most of the time the same results could be achieved no matter the severity of a situation if you just played it straight with them. That's all most of them really wanted, was to be treated fair.

If you promise them a piece of pie, give it to them. If you promise the phones will be on till nine at night don't deviate from that. Note for future administrations: Don't make so many promises!

Speaking of the pie, one day I was in the dining room tower in the cafeteria. The inmate cafeteria is split into three large sections, all visible from the guard tower. Every Thanksgiving, the inmates receive a dinner that rivals the one I eat at home. On this turkey day, the kitchen runs out of pumpkin pie! Eighty-five percent of the prison had received theirs and they have the last of the joint in the inmates dining hall, and then they decide to run out of pie.

First off, most of the inmates probably didn't even want the damn pie. Second, if the clowns did in fact order enough, they might consider letting less walk out of the kitchen! We almost had a riot that day, and I think they bargained the inmates down with some potato chips or something of that nature. The inmates knew the administration would trade for the shortage in some way. Either way though, to make the point quick; the inmates only want what they have coming, nothing more or nothing less.

I think I liked the way prisons used to be run to a certain extent better, because less communication was required. Not to mention the friken politics! Back then the only communication was orders, and that was that. This approach made it much simpler for all concerned. This way an officer could concentrate on his job and all the other bullshit was unnecessary. At the Ville', communication is a tool that has to learned. This was not my doing, and it must have taken a long time to evolve that way. The role of the inmate and officer is so screwed up that either really knows where he stands or what's expected of him for that matter.

The officer of today pays the most. He comes into the system with all his preconceived James Cagney prison movie notions, only to find out that someone in the movies or someone in correctional field fucked up big time! Considering all the ties the prison system has with Hollywood you would think that that just wouldn't happen. The language barrier might even be worse for a new officer that isn't from the city proper. If I guy comes in from the sticks he might as well be listening to French or pig latin because he won't understand shit. Nothing against the French, they probably know how to run their prisons!

Sometimes even if an officer was good at communication, his body language might give him away. The inmates were always looking into your eyes for some sort of sign that your words weren't conveying.

After Sergeant Bigosh left B-East, we acquired the services of a female sergeant named Sergeant Mankee. I would grow to like her very much because she didn't take shit from the inmates. She was a short woman who was short on words also, and didn't seem to have time for any negotiations whatsoever. She was also a petite lady of sorts. The only problem that she had was that she went to that nasty place called disrespect. These inmates as a rule didn't like to take orders anyway. Most of them had obvious tendencies towards being chauvinistic as well, and as such hated being told what to do by her.

One shift in particular stands out. I had been down the flag letting inmates out of their cells and on my way back to the sergeant's office, when I observed her coming out of the sergeant's office with a wooden object of some sort. As I approached I could see she wasn't playing either. An inmate had apparently given her a bit too much shit, and so she was going to deal with it in a Stateville manner. I don't have a doubt in my mind, that if the inmate had taken another step, she would have brained him good.

Luckily two other inmates were holding the inmate back, and the most that actually happened was that they shared a bit of negative vocabulary with each other. Sergeant Mankee became actually good at her job; it's just that sometimes her delivery was a little off. Sergeant Mankee would eventually loose her job after several years putting up with the joint, because she didn't cover here ass on a report. The administration was only worried about how things would play out when an inmate was assaulted. So Sergeant Mankee was the scapegoat. The only thing I can think to say is, if you play with snakes you're probably going get bit. The administration had no loyalty, but to their own.

The inmates had one shower in the cell house to use for personal hygiene. They also used this area for gang meetings, mutual as well as not so mutual sex, and smoking dope. Let me not forget it was also a make shift laundry. Some of the inmates actually washed their clothes while they were still on their backs.

The inmates were opportunists and used every means necessary to survive. I would have to say that even though my job did have a kind of job description, my job was mostly for limiting the previously mentioned inmate opportunities. Correctional Officer as a matter of fact had an exact job description, but I would have to say that at Stateville, If I had went by the letter of those descriptions, I wouldn't be here writing this today.

The inmates had been groomed for a kind of revision of those job descriptions. Trying to complete my job exactly as written was nothing close to practical. What pissed me off was the powers gave me a job to do and told me exactly how to do it, but then changed the rules so those instructions were useless.

I know that if I was the administration, I would give some kind of standard reply to all this, to the effect that "had the officer completed his job as written he would have far less problems". This was a bunch of bullshit though, and I am sure that if I couldn't find at least ten officers working right now to corroborate my story I would eat my badge! Oh shit I gave that back.

I think what this all really comes down to, is officers must deal with more then they really should have to. All the state and the administration cared about was that the prison looked like one. It didn't matter to them if it really functioned like one. What it comes down to is innocent employees and inmates paying for the miss-management of others. WHAT it comes down to is a recipe for Attica soup!

Ok...enough about what I think, what do you think? Shouldn't prisons remain uniform so that everyone knows what their exact function is? Inmates are into words like "routine" not phrases like "new rules" because we fucked up! Inmates don't work well with change, and when an administration is constantly trying to find the right combination to fix an already screwed up environment, that's exactly what they give the inmates.

A good analogy would be that of a renter, whom after many years of the same rent and many years of the same amenities is approached by the warden...oops I mean the landlord, who has a totally new plan. He needs to take back the air conditioning unit, and you would need to start sharing the garage with him. You had been used to the rules for so long; the shock of the new rules really pisses you off. Well of course at this point you would be slightly ticked off and consider a riot...oops I mean a lawyer. Well anyway, I am sure you can see the limited comparison.

Officers were trying to deal with rules that were either not enforced or antiquated altogether. Officers wrote tickets and they were wrong. Officers wrote incident reports and they were wrong. Officers wrote work orders and they were wrong. I was slowly learning that Bigosh was right, do your eight and get the fuck out of there. No waves, no retorts, no opinions...nothing. I don't know; I could be wrong here, but if I were an administrator of anything, the opinions of those on the front lines would be of great use. Considering the varied groups of individuals that worked in B-East, I would have to say that we managed very well some how. Thanks again, to all those I worked with.

Another important aspect of the prison environment is the health care. Rumor had it that more then half the inmates at the penitentiary had A.I.D.S. (acquired immune deficiency syndrome) I'm sure it was easy to acquire too. I knew one inmate that by sight appeared normal except the limited use of a cane. I literally watched him go from that state, to not being able to get out of bed to go to any of the meals. Of course, everyone was notified and he did make some trips to the hospital infirmary, but he remained in B-East till he was pretty much dead.

His brothers would bring him food from the chow hall, even though he rarely ate it. He was prescribed amongst other things, those vitamin drinks such as Insure. Instead of drinking them like he was supposed to, the rumor was he sold them to those inmate types that were into body- building. I guess you might say "oh well that's his problem if he isn't smart enough to drink them himself", but the fact of the matter is if he is sick enough for vitamin supplements and several different medications, he probably is entirely too sick for the general population. I realize I'm not a doctor and I'm not claiming to be, but this inmate and a few others were in population far to long. It's as if they were just housed and it didn't matter where. Many were next to death before they were removed from population. Some of course died before getting to some kind of infirmary.

Lots of times, the inmates would complain about the responsiveness of officers in reference to their health complaints. A lot of the inmates enjoyed playing little games in regards to health though, and this would retard the process a touch. A prime example of that would be when an inmate would complain of chest pains. Well, of course that requires immediate attention and usually medical personnel were called. The snafu here was many times the inmates were playing games to tie up officers, or were just bored and in need of some attention.

Officers I would have to say dealt, with the so called "chest pain" once a shift or so. So this didn't help their attentiveness when it came to medical calls. While I was employed at Stateville, the day shift was the only shift with the proper medical personnel. Since the doctors and or assistants worked the day shift only, any medical technicians that I contacted loved the wild card "There is nothing I can do, have the inmate see the doctor in the morning". If there wasn't blood squirting from their eyes or if they weren't having a major seizure, they might as well tuff it out till the morning.

Hell, there were two med-techs I can think of right of the bat, that I hesitated to call on several occasions because their standard reply to any medical problem was "I can't do shit, have the inmate see the doctor in the morning"! Or "here take these Tylenol". This would do more harm then good and these inmates didn't appreciate total and complete indifference.

Another element of the inmate population was the homosexuals. Some came into the joint already with acquired tastes, and others either acquired the taste while behind the bars or were forced to acquire it. Some were so adept at their craft that they wore woman's panties, nail polish and talked in a distinctly feminine voice. I actually referred to many as she. I know it sounds ridiculous, but when you listen to these umm…convicts on a daily basis and they are continually working on fine-tuning their female characteristics, you would be surprised how easy it is to confuse reality with illusion. Then again I guess they fit right in, because illusion is what Stateville is all about.

As I write this, I continue to wonder how many officers actually paid a price in one way or another for things that could have been easily rectified. I realize that life is a crapshoot anyways, but why do the administrations feel the need to buck the odds? The malevolence that I have towards the state and the administrations while I was there is surely shared by more then I. The employment of course was appreciated; the environment most certainly was not.

Note to future administrations: the ideal prison consists of doors that actually secure. Inmates that don't laugh in your face because they can have a ticket thrown out that you just wrote them, or perhaps brass that stops an inmate for an infraction before he gets to you. Posts that have the needed ammunition to get the job done no matter the scenario and wardens that take reports or work orders seriously. Administrators that have more brains than the convicts would be nice. Ok...Ok... the world isn't a Utopia; I can still dream can't I?

## "The Beginning of the End"

I like to think everything happens for a reason, but at Stateville there was no reason. I was really starting to feel a sickening futility in the cell house after being there for over four years so I decided a change of venue was in order. Some genius had come up with the idea to have a group of officers just for the purpose of assisting the units secure or whatever. Literally a godsend, but than again, I could have told the admin that a crew of that nature was needed along time ago.

I was tired of watching and training officers only to see them leave to another prison or to another profession. The majority of the 1-9 crew, were officers with a background and I felt they seemed pretty united as a team. This in itself appealed to me. They went pretty much together everywhere they went. They were affectionately referred to as "The Lock-Up Crew". These officers literally went from unit to unit assisting the officer's lock-up the respective units. At first I thought this was a fantastic idea, but then as I watched the crew progress in function, I started to notice that inmates were not locking up at all until the crew arrived at a unit to assist. This for the inmates was the time when they felt they HAD to lock up.

So in some ways, even having a crew of with this nature had some faults, because new officers were literally learning their jobs in a less then functional manner. Some were straight up afraid to lock up the inmates themselves until assistance arrived. Before the initiation of the lock-up crew officers had no one to assist him or her, unless of course your unit was lucky enough to have a lieutenant that did his job. The new officers sometimes acted as if they were securing, but in reality they were waiting for the lockup crew to arrive.

As a rule, a unit could be locked up in fifteen minutes or so, so the gallery officers felt, what is the point of my fighting with inmates for an hour or so when the crew would arrive soon anyway, and secure the unit in the blink of an eye. What they didn't realize though, was the crew didn't always show up, and what they didn't realize was, by them waiting they had more or less told the inmates that they couldn't secure a gallery by themselves.

The inmates have nothing better to do then determine an officer's weakness or weaknesses. My weakness was without a doubt kindness. Stateville had unintentionally groomed me to overcome that weakness somewhat though. Well anyway, the officers on the galleries felt they were saving themselves frustration by waiting for the lock up crew, when in effect the were adding to their frustration and didn't even know it at the time.

What I would soon learn was that the lock-up crew would be groomed for other functions. I had the small hope that the administration had put the crew into place for the safety of the institution and to maybe create some good morale amongst the front line employees. What I would find is that slowly we didn't lock up anymore except when we had nothing else to do. We were spending our time relieving officers at towers and such. We also started taking over posts that should have been filled by permanent officers in the first place. All of the assignment changes were of course with the intent to save some dough.

All these new assignments ended up doing was splitting the lockup crew, and taking away from the initial intentions of the crew. I also started to think about what the focus of our little group was. It seemed at the time that a lot of the inmates were complaining about the tactics of the lock up crew as well.

It also became common knowledge that several officers at several different posts were not getting relieved for chow, which by the way, they should have been all along! So here comes the administration again, with another bright idea, and in on fell swoop they take the lock-up crew affectively out of the picture by using them to relieve officers for chow monopolizing the majority of the shift. Saving money and pleasing the inmates all at the same time…in their minds I am sure they felt they had achieved administrative nirvana!

We were used for so many assignments, that actually I liked it personally because being in the cell house for so long didn't give me much of a chance to check out the other posts in the prison. We were used for whatever the wardens could come up with. So we slowly became the jack-of-all-trades and no longer the master of one.

For a while we did have a legitimate purpose, and I think we were a morale booster. We were usually about ten to twelve officers strong with two or three whiteshirts. The whiteshirts complained about us being pretty much neutered and then they found themselves also being used for relief work as well.

Because Stateville was so screwed up, we usually spent the first two hours of hour shift running around the entire prison trying to put inmates back in their respective units or assignments. The prison is rather large and two hours is somewhat a long period of time, so many times we would chase a group from State and Madison* or out of the tunnels, and by the time we made our rounds and returned to the original point, those same inmates would be right back were they were chased from in the first place!

At least before they split us up we were getting some respect from the inmates. We would walk into a unit and the inmates almost ran towards their cells. I do realize of course this was respect due to the size of our group. Along with the cell house personnel, we pretty much never had a problem. That irritated the inmates and slowly we as a driving force became non-existent; literally as far as the cell houses were concerned. Some of us were relieving towers or other posts and some of us were dealing with the visiting room or writs*. They had us in the tunnels for a while trying to control movement a bit. When we started doing that too effectively, that also became "off limits", the same as the cell houses had become.

A new job we acquired was the running of the circle*. This job pretty much entailed watching as the units came into the dining hall one by one and received the evening meal. We also were supposed to keep an eye on the kitchen help, so they didn't steal food from the kitchen. FAT CHANCE!

The administration also came up with the bright idea for night visits. DO you believe that?! Like the inmates didn't have enough privileges already. Guess who the obvious choice was for running those visits?

So here we were running visits, running the circle, and relieving towers. So because the inmates didn't like the fact that the prison was starting to run a little bit like a real prison, we were pretty much barred from the cell houses or the tunnels and instead were all split into groups and dealt with a myriad of tasks appearing all the time to have a legitimate function, but rendering us useless as a group.

As far as watching the kitchen went, the inmates had been stealing food for so long, the new concept of officers stopping them damn near started several riots. I wish I had a nickel for every time we almost ended up in a serious situation over food. You have to understand I don't blame the inmates at all for this either. All they were doing was the same thing they had been allowed to do for who knows how many years. You must also understand that these inmates were probably stealing the food for their chief or to pay dues or debts. They had become accustomed to getting what they wanted, and they also knew their chief or the people they owed wouldn't take any excuses. So I do understand why we had all the problems. What I don't understand is how we made it without more officers getting hurt over this shit.

The officers that paid though were those same officers that had gotten so used to us entering the unit and securing. Now all they had was themselves and the inmates. Not a good scenario, given the fact they had made it clear to the inmates what their individual personality traits were from the start, by waiting for other officers to assist them.

On the subject of the inmates in the kitchens; should they even be there in the first place? Should inmates with life sentences be able to touch food eaten by inmates and officers? Should they be around knives as long as your forearm? I would think not. Than again it's a money thing I guess. Safety of residents and staff comes in second to saving a buck. Note to future administrations: Hire outside people to prepare the food at the maximum-security level. The money you save in stolen food will more then likely make up for the extra staff. Heck, you might even come out in the plus column with that deal.

The kitchens did have an entity known as food supervisor. I guess they figured it was better to give the food up rather then be assaulted or maybe they were on the take, who knows? Either way, they either were allowing the food to be stolen, or they simply turned their heads, which pretty much amounts to the same thing. The only thing I figured they were supervising was the continual illegal depletion of the state food. At one point there was even a female supervisor that was giving the inmates more then food. Well, she eventually was caught and was fired of course, but if the inmates weren't in the kitchen in the first place, all these problems could have been avoided.

Again, I don't blame the inmates because they do what they are allowed to get away with. Stealing food was an "allowed endeavor" for so long the inmates felt this was like a perk at a job. The same old predicament occurred though when the administration decided enough was enough. The officers were put in the middle. I especially felt sorry for the new officers that were assigned cell house door assignments.

I recall the 1-9 lock-up crew being called to the various unit doors to quell many an argument over nothing any more serious then some overdone hamburgers. Of course there were officers and/or brass in between the kitchen and the unit doors, but how can someone effectively stop someone from an undertaking that has been part of the itinerary for so long? I felt bad myself trying to stop these guys. Not scared mind you...bad! For years, they're more or less allowed to take what they want to the units, and then the administration gets some unexpected squeezing from the powers down state about the bullshit, and then wham; you have officers at risk over some burgers, Because now THEY want to try and run things they way it should have been done all along.

When the brass in the tunnels were questioned why they let food go by, they loved the standard answer "they were testing the door officers to see if they would perform their assignments correctly." Give me a break! Not all brass behaved this way, but some were so pissed at the 180-degree turn the administration took in regards to security that they themselves felt put on the hot seat. I know I don't want to die over a few chicken breasts, so who could blame them actually.

I too was wrong on many occasions and eventually turned my job on and off like the others, because I was taught that way. On one particular shift I was heading to the officers chow hall with an upset stomach. Probably from the crap I was ingesting to begin with! I get to the chow hall and there are inmates from my unit behind the counter serving the officers food. I tell inmate so and so, "hey look, my stomach is pretty upset so go ahead and give me like three pieces of white meat and forget the other stuff." By rights we were supposed to get one piece of chicken and a varied supply of side orders.

I had pissed him off somewhere along the line so he says "the supervisor says play it by the book tonight we don't have enough to go around". Well of course I know he is full of shit, and so I eat the crap he gives me. I was hungry, but sick at the same time, so while I'm devouring my ration I devise a plan. The problem here as I saw it, was an inmate trying to use rules he didn't go by in the first place, in an attempt to piss me off. This inmate had been working at the kitchen a long time and made it a nightly ritual to come to the unit loaded down with goodies. As I said this was the usual for the inmates, and they looked at it as an added benefit to their jobs. He had to go by several gates and personnel to get to the unit, but it was always the same, arrive with a whole boatload and sell it in the cell house.

Well, I knew when he would arrive approximately, and so I relieved the door officer. I decided this would be a good time to go by the rules as well. As I am looking down the tunnel, I see the usual sight. Several kitchen workers heading toward the unit door loaded down with stolen food. They enter the interlock and I do the most disgraceful thing I ever did while employed for the state. I allow every inmate in the unit with the food except one. Wrong I know, and about as low as you can get on a professional level. I was focused nonetheless. I started shaking the inmate down and order him to give me the contraband food. He of course laughs in a matter a fact way, saying what's up officer, you let the others through.

I pull a sack with like a dozen breasts from under his coat and he is about ready to go to knuckle junction. Obviously earlier when he said the chicken was short, it was because the inmates had to get their cut first. He grabs the sack back in a "fuck you" kind of way and I call the unit lieutenant to the door. All the time not opening the door, he is stuck in the interlock. He's cussing up a storm and threatening me, and just then the lieutenant shows up. This guy is going on and on about the other inmates going through and the fact that I am playing favorites and the like. I of course had explained the situation to the white shirt prior to the scheduled event and besides the lieutenant had seen this crap before. The inmate would eventually throw the chicken to the floor, and stomp on it while arguing at the same time, about who should have it.

I know he felt I wanted the chicken, but that wasn't it. My having the chicken was of no consequence. I felt the need to use the system to my benefit, just like everyone else was doing. I realize you the reader should stop reading right here do to the integrity issue, but keep in mind this was a point in my career that I had seen enough. To this day, feel bad about this incident, but I would be amiss not to give you the whole story. I felt that if I didn't do something, that my credibility as an officer would have went right down the tubes. The other inmates knew he fucked me back at the kitchen and they probably had a nice laugh. In the end, the white shirt felt I was right, although he was a bit concerned about my tactics. I would normally not be a person to retaliate in that fashion. I was only doing what had been for so long, drilled into my head. Cover your ass, because we won't, and do what ever you have to do to survive in this "rules apply sometimes" penal colony!

Technically, I could have had him fired from his job with a violation report, but I felt the creative correction technique was good enough. Besides, with a little maneuvering, he more than likely would have had his job back anyway.

"Creative corrections" was a mandatory part of an officer's repertoire if he or she expected to survive. The inmates knew the usual avenues were pretty much worthless. If it would get around through the inmate population that you would do whatever it took to do your job, you were already a step ahead of the rest. Utilizing those creative procedures was all part of the Stateville game. Not wanting to admit it, passing these tests was similar to the tests the inmates had to pass to survive. I belonged at Stateville as an officer when I walked in the door. By the time I would resign I most certainly didn't! I had become the problem and not the solution, but at least I guess, I'm here to tell the story.

Well enough about food, back to the lock-up crew. As I was saying before, the 1-9 lock-up crew was a good concept that became distorted. At the beginning of the lock up crew inception, they would return to units for a second or third time to re-secure the units. Partly because the officers were not doing there jobs and partially because the inmates could kick out of their cells. The doors in B-West had been redone with new locks but B-East didn't secure for shit, so we actually were going around in circles looking like we were doing something, but not accomplishing very much.

The doors were originally hydraulic in nature many years before. Somewhere along the line that system was circumvented. They used the side locks and the lock boxes at the end of the galleries for securing. Eventually the inmates would file of the latches on the doors enough, so that they wouldn't do their jobs and the kick outs were everywhere.

Eventually the administration started to feel the heat from the less then adequate cell doors, and after years of neglect decided on a top lock system. This system would entail more or less a lock on the top of each cell that rendered kick outs a dieing art. At first a godsend, it had its faults as well. I found myself needing a milk crate to stand on, in order to open the doors successfully. This kind of takes away from my effectiveness as a gallery officer wouldn't you say?

The inmates in B-east became more violent the longer I stayed at the Ville', but the administration decided B-West would be the first renovation project. I thought that the flow of construction from B-West to B-East would be pretty much non-stop. Again I was wrong. There was a lengthy period between the two projects. This made it exceptionally hard on the B-East officers. Not because the inmates could get out as usual, but because they knew their time was short in respect to the ripping and running. The lock-up crew started to be the B-East crew for a time. The doors on the west side were working for the most part and the attitude of the east side inmates was, "go ahead and secure me, I'll just kick out." So the lock up crew spent a good majority of time over there before they were sent to the other assignments mentioned earlier.

This all goes to preventive medicine. I remember a distinct incident where right after the B-West renovation had finally been completed, an argument started on the B-East side. I was on the catwalk and an inmate on the front of eight gallery was refusing to lockup. The situation wouldn't appear as a problem at first glance because ninety percent of the gallery was visually secured. The officer called a white shirt to assist in the lockup. Like a staged play, the entire front of eight gallery started to kick out of their cells in force.

Angry inmates all of a sudden blocked in the few officers on the gallery from both sides. I, as well as my partner fired warning shots into the ceiling. Almost as if someone had prayed on queue, several whiteshirts ran up the stairs and diplomacy somehow brought the situation back to normal. Luckily the situation turned out the way it did, with no one hurt. It's just that these situations played out constantly, with the odds against us. We were always trying to beat the clock. If the doors worked properly to begin with, the shots would not have been fired and the inmates would have remained in their cells. The officer could have waited all day for a whiteshirt to assist. With the doors the way the were, time was always an enemy.

I remember the morale of the officers being extremely low. It was hard to do your job because no one gave a fuck. Everyone felt the same way; the apathy on the part of the administration did nothing less then spread like a cancer. The officers did what they had to do to survive. Rules incessantly were retooled to appropriate a given situation.

The officers were constantly having conversations in regards to rule changes and things getting fixed. I am sure that other professions have similar gripes and concerns, but again mistakes in our world could be nothing less then catastrophic in nature for those in the wrong place at the wrong time. There was no room for indifference; but yet we dealt with the indifference shift after shift not unlike a reoccurring terrible nightmare.

Another of the genius ideas brought on by an administration trying to correct its own mistakes was having the lock-up crew shake down every inmate they came across between one and three in the afternoon. The conundrum here was that "the powers that be shouldn't be" couldn't decide what actual function they wanted the lock-up boys to accomplish in the first place. Ok let me see here…they have to look like their doing something, but yet we don't want them annoying the inmates. Strange concept really, considering the atmosphere. This misconstrued strategy always put us on the hot seat.

One day on State and Madison, we came across the Vice Lord chief from B-West and about six to eight of his cronies. We of course decided this group needed shaking down, since they looked as though they were running the place with their "Don't fuck with us stride". Plus this was part of our "NEW" orders shaking down inmates that we came across while making rounds. As they came closer, we told main control to secure the door at State and Madison. This pretty much stopped them in their tracks. We were about nine officers strong and we had one captain. As they approached, we announced this was a shakedown. Yea right! They literally refused, saying more or less that we would have to force the ordeal. Well, obviously this was a clue for even the less then intelligent, that they were loaded down with weapons.

For a few moments we just stood there like an impotent boyfriend hoping that somehow he would get laid. I noted the time as being 2:35pm. The majority of the 3-11 shift would be walking in the door for roll call and the entire staff of 7-3 where still on the grounds. The whiteshirt that had charge of us in an attempt to make a statement ordered the two towers that had a visual on us to prepare for anything. I noticed that main control didn't say a thing in reference to this order. I could see the officers were worried because of the lack of aggressiveness by the captain. The inmates of course looked as though they had already won the battle.

The inmates just stood there waiting for us to do our job. We didn't. The Captain decided to have a little pow-wow with chief and the two sides just stood there for about ten minutes trying to look like they each was in control. While I was standing there looking at best stupid, I tried to visualize the potential scenarios that could become of this mutual neutralization.

Suddenly, as if out of nowhere, the whiteshirt orders the door on State and Madison opened and the inmates go through, like we were just checking identification or something. The inmates walked past us with a less then respectful gait. I knew the officers were pissed, because I was fuming. We all went back to the shift captains' office, and before the captain had a chance to explain her motives, I run my mouth about our crew being worthless. I didn't know she was on the other side of the door and then she walks in with this, "I wanted everyone to go home philosophy". So now it's the captains views versus officer Thomas' views. I really think, this was the point when I knew I wouldn't make it as a correctional officer.(did I say that already?) The captain had a valid point and we all did go home safely at the end of the shift. Still, to this day, I wonder how many people were stabbed with the same weapons we should have confiscated. I try not to think of the potential fallout due to our lack of action that day because I have a hard enough time dealing with actual memories much less potential ones. Hypothetical scenarios are not my favorite pastime.

That brings to mind, my favorite all time lock up crew embarrassment. Not long after the top locks had gone in at B-West, we were locking up the institution in our usual futile manner, when the powers that shouldn't be, decided on a new plan. We as a lock up crew as a rule locked up all the units, pretty much entirely. Except the B-West Flag (1Gallery), which by past practice had a default visa when it came to lockup. I was never really sure why one gallery had this permanent right, but so it was.

On this particular shift, we were going to make a stand. I guess, even the folks that had engineered this joke of political genius had had enough. Well anyway, the lock-up crew was to report to the B-West sergeant's office. When we arrived I was surprised to see what appeared to be about every available body in the entire institution. I knew something pretty big was up, as I surveyed the situation and counted approximately twenty to twenty five green-shirts* and about a half dozen whiteshirts. I thought damn; whatever we are about to do must surely be something of a large scale, and with the personnel standing around I felt fairly comfortable.

The administration had decided with a lot of nudging from the B-West staff that it was time for the "Prima Donna" types to be treated just like the other inmates in the institution. At this point, I had been at the penitentiary for about six years and had never seen B-West flag locked up completely. Of course on lockdowns they would lock up, but on nightly basis they had the run of the unit pretty much. The other units on the other hand at least had a couple rules they had to go by. This wasn't the case with the B-West boys, and they had become accustomed to their roaming ways.

So it wasn't very surprising that I didn't have a clue as to our intentions when I arrived at B-West. It was, as a matter of fact a rather large surprise to hear we were implementing an alteration of the usual policy.

Consequently, we are instructed that EVERYONE would be locking up on the first pass and this would be the procedure from now on. I should have known right from the start that this was probably the biggest joke to date, but after hearing the plans I was in my usual state of "it was about time we did something constructive" mode.

As a group, we began walking on the flag like we owned the joint (which is the way it should have been all along). We walk the length of the flag and begin locking cells up from the far end towards the front of the unit. Everything seemed to be running really well until we got to about the fire escape in the middle of the gallery. All of a sudden as quickly as we started, we stop cold turkey and stand still. No one is moving at all, except the group of whiteshirts approaching a certain chief living at that exact location.

So slowly, the entire group of security begins to congregate about ten yards from the discussion point. We stand and wait for like fifteen minutes while the whiteshirts have a bit of a pow-wow with the chief in question. I was standing wondering about the State and Madison incident and what had become of that, when I noticed the whiteshirts motion to the officers to unlock the entire group of doors we had just previously secured. I couldn't believe what a big deal was made of this event, and the futility of the final outcome. We looked like such fools walking off the flag that day with our tails between our legs, and all the inmates still out and unsecured. I think even the inmates were a bit shocked, since I didn't hear a lot of laughing coming from the galleries.

Ok, lets see, we had about thirty to thirty-five staff and two shotguns. There were approximately seventy inmates assigned to one gallery, and some of those had been locked up. I don't intend to sit here and try and determine the odds on the outcome of an all out brawl, and I don't believe that our trying to take control by force was the wise move either. Yet, it would seem reasonable to me that if I was going to attempt to take control of a given cell house and I was going to send this many officers to that cell house in an attempt to make a stand, that a possible, if not probable scenario would be the chief in the middle of the gallery saying something to the effect "Kiss my ass!" What else is he going to say; he knows the administration blinks all the time, why should this time be any different.

More then likely the conversation that took place with the whiteshirts was something to the effect of "Would you please like up"? The more then likely reply was "No, I don't think so". That's when we exited the unit, like a bunch of officers at the wrong prison. Note to future administrations: If your foolish enough to make deals with the inmates in the first place and you do decide to eventually take back a prison metaphorically speaking, Make sure you cover at least the obvious scenarios so you don't look foolish. The chief saying "NO" would be a probable scenario, and as such you should be prepared to meet that answer. Let's say it isn't clever to risk the officer's lives trying to enforce your mistakes. Well, then you should have had a sizable tactical team ready to go in case of such a scenario. You increase the catwalk and go in and save some face. You don't have the officers go in the unit with an obvious mission, and let them walk back out the same way they entered with nothing accomplished!

The same would apply to the State and Madison incident and many others that would take another whole book to convey. If for any reason, the inmates won't cooperate with the usual staff, you drop whatever your doing and you deal with that matter directly. If it takes hours to put together a multi-institutional tactical team or whatever, you deal with it. Money isn't always the prime concern. When the administrations and the state finally figure that out, maybe some enduring changes can really be made. I have this haunting nightmare that whenever an incident occurs, the first question relating to that incident is, what are we going to tell Springfield, and what is the projected cost.

For the sake of argument, if a prison is run with the rules applying in all units on a daily basis, it's not unreasonable to believe that money might actually be saved in the long run. As mentioned earlier, the prison system isn't supposed to be run as a profitable venture. No matter how hard you try, your not going to come out in the black at the end of the year.

I remember another time when we were locking up B-West and there was a storm kicking serious ass outside. We had ninety percent of the unit secure and were about ready to leave the unit. Suddenly the lights go out and we are left on the galleries trying to fumble with those glorious padlocks at the end of, and in the middle of each gallery. Fumbling with the locks wasn't really the big deal because our eyes did adjust pretty quickly, but B-West had so many inmates assigned to erroneous jobs that it literally left plenty of manpower unsecured to do any damage that might at anytime be called for. The outage only lasted a couple of minutes, but long minutes they were. Each gallery had about six or so inmates allowed to be out and the flag of course was open.

I really got a kick out of B-West really. They had by far the most inmates assigned to cell house duties, but yet it was the filthiest unit in the joint. I'm talking the real type of filthy; "the kind where you go all the way home after your shift, and shower like hell, and still feel your skin crawling kind."

Another story about B-West comes to mind. I had decided to stay for the midnight shift and make some extra cash. I am assigned the B-West catwalk and I am instructed that no one is to be out on the flag due to a recent lockdown. Well, you remember that Lieutenant I told you I worked for in H-House and then again in B-East? Don't laugh; but he was promoted to Captain. Well he is the same individual that is assigned as the shift captain on this particular shift. Maybe it was for the best that he acquired the captains' bars. Considering he had fucked up a lot in the past maybe this was a way he could mask his incompetence just a bit better.

Lets see; I'm on the catwalk like fifteen minutes and I look down on the flag and there are like eight inmates playing cards at two tables. WE ARE ON LOCDOWN! So I do as instructed, and I inform Stateville base that inmates are out on the flag in B-West. Actually the proper thing was to inform the B-West sergeant and then he could do what he felt was appropriate. This was the proper move by me in this case though, because if I had notified the B-West sergeant directly, he would have told me not to worry about it, or do a 434 or something else as useless. Besides, if I told base what was happening, the transmission went over the institutional channel rather then just the house channel. More then likely something would get done. I always was forever hoping something would get done somewhere.... anywhere.

To my surprise, here comes Captain I-think-I-can. Wearing his newly found badge along with what appeared to be his newly found balls. Just like Stateville inevitability, I watched as he spoke a few words, patted a certain high ranking inmate on the back a few times in a take care gesture and walked back out the same way he had come in. leaving the inmates right where he found them sitting at the table playing cards.

I guess he had the bars, but no balls after all. Well the night went ok I guess; the inmates would eventually go into their individual cells at their leisure. Again though, everyone went home safe and no harm done, right? All that can be said is pretty fucking sad huh? Stateville rules were easy to understand I guess, leave us alone and we leave you alone. Of course the inmates were the ones who incorporated this rule, with everyone complying in full.

I would love to tell you a happy story, but the only one I can think of is when I finally resigned.

I really had no problem putting my little ass on the line to change things, but I just wanted to be sure others were on the same page, so I wasn't attempting this futile venture alone. The only ones that were on the same page as I saw it; were the chiefs and the administration. When the chiefs cried, something was done. When the staff cried, the administration said let us validate things with the chiefs first.

The funny thing about Stateville was…Well…I guess I should have said ANOTHER funny thing about Stateville was that the state performed the executions there. Not that execution is funny, but I think they could have saved an exorbitant amount of negative publicity, not to mention the forever sought after dollar if they just incorporated a new practice regarding the condemned. How you say? Dress the condemned in an officer's uniform and send him on the galleries with the understood authority to lock-up everyone. I think this is how I, and many of my co-workers felt on a daily basis; like a condemned person just waiting for the big moment! See what I mean about my humor? I not long ago, laughed at jokes much less disturbing.

Note to future administrations: I was only kidding about the dress em' up in an officer's uniform thing!

Probably the most infamous mass murderer put to death at Stateville was John Wayne Gacy. He was put to death for the murder of thirty-three young men. I do have mixed emotions about the death penalty in general, but if anyone deserved it, ole' Johnny was it. The execution night was always a fiasco to a certain extent, with press everywhere and tons of right to lifers with their candles singing or chanting "anti-death penalty" jargon. This execution had much more publicity though. Executions were customarily performed at midnight in X-House. Illinois had long since converted from the electric chair to lethal injection.

I didn't mind execution nights except that the dignitaries that attended theses functions used the officer's dining room for their meal. The officers would use the inmate's kitchen, which I didn't like very much. I usually didn't eat on these nights, and all I would think about as my stomach did it's usual growling was the birthday party like atmosphere around the officers dining room and the feast inside. The officers were not allowed to partake in the specially preferred buffet.

I also didn't savor eating in the inmate's kitchen due to the usual intense looks by the inmates preparing the food. I am relatively sure they didn't like the concept of the state waxing one of their own, and I decided these were not good nights to be eating food served by pissed of felons.

Another note of amusement was the ritual by which we prepared for the big day. Usually the entire week before an execution or the visit of a downstate big wig, the inmates cleaned their asses off to make the joint look much more acceptable then the usual day to day filth fest. They would clean; wax, mop or paint; whatever was needed to camouflage the usual appearance of the place.

In all, about ten convicts would be put to death during my stay at the Ville'. One night they even conducted a double execution.

On a lighter side, holidays at Stateville were interesting. On Christmas for example, the inmates received a nice meal along with a bag delivered to their cells with candy and a couple packs

141

of cigarettes. I was always wondering when they would make us dress like Santa Claus to deliver those bags.

Thanksgiving was a feast for the inmates in that they received everything from turkey to pumpkin pie and everything in between. Of course on the holidays more food was available, making for more deals and theft. I do like the time they ran out of pumpkin pie. We had completed feeding the entire institution, except for one unit. The inmates were about the rip the place apart over one piece of pumpkin pie! I was assigned the DRT* that day and I thought for sure I was going to have to shoot an inmate or two. Luckily the whiteshirts bargained with the pumpkin pie craving cons and we eventually gave up a couple little bags of chips and some ice cream to each resident. As usual the babies would get their way, and we all went home safe. It doesn't matter if the cooking staff miss-ordered the pie or if it was stolen (which is the most likely scenario) if you promise these guys something, you had better come up with it. The problem arises again that the individual that fucked up this state of affairs was not the one that had to rectify it…and so it went. Whoops, I told you that story. I at least embellished a bit.

On the fourth of July if you were a prisoner assigned one of the upper tiers in any of the units, you could probably see the fireworks coming from the local festivals. This also applied to the officers that were lucky enough to get wall towers as their afternoon assignment.

As far as Halloween was concerned, guess it would suffice to say that I always felt somewhat in costume anyway. It also seemed as though the inmates as a group were a lot more active in a mischievous way when the moon was full. This could have been my imagination given the somewhat tenuous atmosphere behind the walls, but most other officers felt the same way.

Several movies have been done at Stateville: Weeds, Gabriel's Fire, and Natural Born Killers to name a few. Oh yes, I was supposed to have had you do your own research on that. Well there were more then those three so happy hunting.

Although an effective backdrop for these moneymaking ventures, is this place the proper venue where movies should be filmed? Considering that Hollywood can pretty much construct whatever they want and/or use computers to create whatever environment they want, the only thing I can think of is it is about money once again. Why else would the state put so many people at risk?

Natural Born Killers was filmed at Stateville for pretty much an entire summer. I was assigned the lock-up crew when they filmed, and we spent the summer escorting movie types all around the compound. They even went as far as to use actual inmates in the production. During a riot scene, an actor had his jaw broke by an inmate so the administration and movie moguls decided they shouldn't use inmates any longer. I guess that's why they make the big bucks anyway, to make decisions that should have been apparent in the first place. The real problem with hordes of movie equipment and movie people running everywhere was that we continued to run the prison as usual. They might be filming in the tunnel and we would be moving lines of convicts to the chow hall or to a program. The inmates were constantly coming into direct contact with people from the outside.

I remember looking down from an upper gallery in B-West while we were moving a chow line. On the flag far below they were filming a scene and proportionately there was well over two-dozen people involved and yards of high voltage cables. As I walked I noticed a couple different mop buckets filled with water. I can only imagine if an inmate would have kicked a bucket or two over the side of the gallery. I am still surprised to this day that the inmates didn't try taking hostages or something even more vile. This of course would have made for an even better movie.

While they filmed they were using prop shotguns and such. What if a major insurrection had occurred? It would have gotten complicated real fast. With all those people running around with fake shotguns, dressed in convict and or officer attire I don't even want to contemplate potential scenarios or outcomes. Note to future administrations: NO movies people; at least not at the max joints. It doesn't matter if the film industry buys you new lighting for the tunnels or we get to meet some actors (which was kind of cool), Business of any type other then corrections itself should not even be an option. You people have enough to worry about in the first place.

Before you start expanding your horizons, try putting together a solid itinerary that can't be ridiculed because of obvious shortcomings. When you get that completed, then think…yes think, about other ventures.

Recently a super-max was completed downstate. I have mixed emotions about this site as well. While employed as an officer one thing I would pray for was a super max in hopes we would have some leverage on these inmates. Rumor has it that the inmates spend twenty plus hours in there cells. If I was still working for the Illinois Department of Corrections I would probably jump up and down yelling "It's about time they got hard nosed with these felons".

The thing is this; if the maximum institutions had been run properly from the start, the state probably could have saved a fortune by not having to construct this super maximum facility. As it is now, they send incorrigibles there as punishment. You might wonder to yourself what is wrong with that, since all prison systems have their fair share of clowns.

I do like the fact the state took a proactive status in regards to the inmate behavioral problems and at the same time gave employees a little definitive power. Or is it proactive in the first place? The riddle here is that there state continues to fumble around without an exact plan of attack. Choosing instead to deal with problems that become too much of a burden to them or start to become a cancer in relation to press releases and the like. Anything that doesn't give them a headache directly or doesn't make it to the papers is considered daily fodder.

It's really easy for papers to get lost or for people to forget. If it happened yesterday its old news, so sweep it under the rug! Hell, the papers didn't find out about it, so that at least will suffice. Of course I'm talking in generalities here. I wish I new ten percent of the crap that was hushed. Actually re-thinking that comment, maybe I don't!

## "Memories to Last a Lifetime"

I know I have already conveyed to you many of my personal views and given you a somewhat cursory viewing of Stateville, but I have a few tidbits left that have some relevance or are just plain favorite stories. Actually maybe more soapbox or rambling thoughts, but if you've mad it this far, you will find the rest at worst a bit interesting.

I would eventually leave the lock-up crew and go where all burnouts went; the midnight shift. I too had become the problem in my own way and was less then effective as an officer during my last couple years of employment. I was so stressed trying to make some kind of sense about this place that the eleven to seven shift was my only choice. I had heard that on that shift you basically only interacted with the inmates for a couple hours at the end of the shift and it was considered to be pretty much a cakewalk.

When I bumped to the midnight shift I found it kind of ironic I would end up at the place that I had started… H-House. Kind of poetic actually, like a mouse in a maze looking for the lone piece of cheese. Well, since the pastime on the midnight shift was for officers to sleep as much as possible, the officers actually had two different assignments during the shift to split it up a bit. I guess the hope being at least the change in venue would have the propensity to wake them up.

The midnight shift would report for roll call at 10:45 and usually the inmates were pretty tired out by that point and the only responsibility we really had was the feeding in the morning and the few morning details we had to let out for work. So the optimum situation if you were as burned out as I was, was to get one of the towers for the second half of the shift so that you didn't have to deal directly with the inmates at all.

Well as usual Officer Thomas was assigned the tower for the first half and H-House for the second half of the shift. Still not a bad deal, considering I used to deal with the convicts for eight hours. At this point in my juncture though, even two hours was hell, and shit the inmates were even sleepy and less then aggressive to say the least. All they wanted to do usually was get their breakfast and go back to bed.

I thought I might have found a good place to "do my eight and go home" as Bigosh would say. I also found myself with the exact state of mind that he said I would eventually achieve. I didn't give a fuck just like the curriculum had intended. I too had become exactly what I had disliked about so many of the old timers many years before. I would watch the new officers come through the door in their newly pressed shirt and pants ready to rock the world, and I was thinking pretty much the same way that Sergeant Bigosh did years before in B-East.

In the tower on the first half of the shift, I found my self with many hours to contemplate my time and futility at Stateville. I had watched people come and go both as inmates and as officers. I noticed that the percentage that left in one piece or with full mental faculties functioning properly was most certainly a small minority. I also noticed that the few that would remain after my departure; and had in fact persevered at least as long as I, were a select few who either decided to put up with the shit for the income or where those who this environment suited anyway. I was neither of those, and was apparently more human then I really care to admit. I am sorry to say I do have a breaking point, and I did not have the determination to continue kicking and scratching with the hope of a final redemption that I finally learned would never come.

There were times on the eleven to seven shift where I felt a received a bit of a break and was assigned one of the two roving officer spots. One officer was assigned the north portion of the institution and the other was assigned the south end. Well at least with this assignment I could more or less come and go at my leisure except for running lines in the morning. I also was expected to make rounds in the different buildings on the institutional grounds. I can tell you that walking in a very large building that seems to talk to you when the wind blows is a very interesting thing. By yourself and expected to completely check the entire building. This included the basement and main floors.

The same could be said for the tunnels that run all along the institution to many different locations. Those tunnels were hot and humid because they had so many pipes and leakage from above ground. The also had their own set of ominous noises. If you really had the willies you might come across the occasional skunk rounding a corner unexpectedly just for effect. Working the midnights at this joint defiantly was an eye opener.

The Monkeys on my back had clawed relentlessly, knowing all along of the eventuality of the inevitability to come. I of course like many others before me, choose to believe we could fight an ineffectual war and win. Note to current and future correctional officers: If your there for the eight and the benefits, stay; if your there thinking you can make a difference, leave as soon as possible! I'm not being melodramatic with this statement. Either you belong there or you don't. A simple way to determine that, is to decide right up front if you're the kind of person that can close your eyes and turn off all your other senses at a moments notice. If you're that kind of person, by all means become a correctional officer. If on the other hand, improprieties and futility are distasteful to you, even in the least bit, consider another vocation!

I really hate making that statement, because when I started at the penitentiary it would have aggravated the shit out of me! Guess that is what happens to a wanna' be idealist. It's kind of like waking from a great dream, to a cold wet morning with an unwanted reality staring you in smack dab right in the face.

Memories are funny things; over time they're like an ever-changing cloud formation. Always there, but always appearing at a slightly different perspective at the very same time. Concerning my aptitude to recall those memories in a fair manner, I would have to say that recollections from Stateville are slightly more indelible then average everyday reminiscences. They have a way of permeating your very being in a very clear and merciless manner. The powers that be, will of course attempt as usual to play political games and try to take away from the validity of the words printed here. They don't want to go to that arena. The only suggestion I do have is learn by your mistakes for once, and move on. As Ozzy would put it, "this is your "Crazy Train" baby, I'm getting off!

The words here are for quick reference to be used by the future administrations. Those that forget the past are surely destined to repeat it! …I know I'm rambling again, so let me tell you a few stories that might amuse you or possibly disgust you, depending on your personal makeup.

The lock-up crew was at the end of one of our shifts and counting the minutes before we would eventually leave, when we were called again to the wonderful world of B-West. It seems an inmate had overdosed and we were to shake down his cell in an attempt to ascertain why. By the time we had completely turned the cell upside down, we had found a large amount of drugs and cash. The logical thing to assume at this point was that he was a dealer and that several other convicts also had their hands on what appeared to be a bad concoction of heroin. Before we could say "reality what a concept" several inmates were requesting a medical technician. Before the night would end, the three local emergency rooms would be jam packed with inmates from Stateville Correctional Center complaining of a wide assortment of ailments. It was a mad house to say the least. The entire front of the prison was a sea of ambulances and emergency vehicles. Every inmate that went to the hospital had to be escorted. The rule of thumb of course was two officers per inmate when being escorted past the confinement of the walls, but here again we circumvented procedure. I am relatively sure each inmate had one officer assigned. I do know for a fact when I arrived at the hospital emergency room with my convict in tow, that the room was full and very few officers were there, one per inmate at best. I believe that for any high escape risks that made the trip to the hospital, they actually did have two officers accompany them.

Some genius had at least called the State Police and they were there already when I arrived. This was a good thing, since we had not only left the grounds at one inmate per officer but also left without side arms. I remember thinking, what if one of these inmates is only playing with us, and looking for quick exit. The lucky thing, (and many times Stateville did have that) was that nothing did transpire and all inmates were treated with out incident.

On another glorious occasion, it had gotten around the prison grapevine that a gun was in the institution and it wasn't in the possession of the security staff either. Apparently this scared the wardens enough that they actually tracked it down. How they received the information one can only contemplate, but it would become common knowledge that it was finally located buried by the theatre building. Upon discovery, it was learned that it was a fully functional, loaded thirty-eight. It was completely oiled and in a condom. Only god and a few others know how it actually ended up behind the walls, but inmates had been known to stick objects as large as a gun up their ass holes. I wonder how many more weapons are there or will be there because of continued head turning on the part of the shot callers. No pun intended.

I do have to say that the state has made some halfhearted attempts to change the system as a whole. There have in fact been some changes made for the better since I left. I can only hope and pray for the employees, that the state decides that maybe running the prison system in a reasonably effective manner might save them some money and they will continue on the road to a safer environment for all concerned. One only has to read the papers from the past ten years in reference to some events that have transpired in the system to determine whatever their doing now is definitely not working and changes have got to be made. As an addendum to that statement; keep in mind, that probably ninety percent of all the bullshit that goes on behind the walls never reaches the media.

That actually goes back to the statement a new officer signs concerning confidentiality. I realize some things need to be kept in the profession, but this confidentiality statement is clearly for the assumed safety of the brass. It has nothing to do with security in general, since the state has no problems with tour groups or dignitaries or movie people for that matter, completely viewing or filming the entire institution!

Since we are on the subject of institutional security or lack there of, I would really be amiss if I failed to mention the infamous Speck tapes. The state's worse nightmare came true when someone sneaked a VHS recorder into the institution (imagine that!) and did an unauthorized interview with none other then Richard Speck. The tapes bring to light the true Stateville in all its glory.

In the tapes, Speck sits with a buddy bragging about the life he has behind bars. He mentions everything from the availability of drugs, to the sex, to his king like status and understood authorization to freely roam the prison grounds. (Under the guise of a prison painter of course) It showed a boastful Speck with female breasts sitting in woman's panties. He was said to say "if they knew the fun I am having they would set me free!" This enlightening recording found its way to the media and the state officials on or about May of 1996. The funny thing was, Speck died just one day shy of his 50th birthday on December fifth of 1991, almost five years prior. Where was this tape being held all this time and why wasn't it presented much earlier? It took this event for state officials to even begin to take notice of the mayhem at Stateville, it's a shame it wasn't presented much earlier.

Well of course, there was a big to do about the whole thing and there were high-level discussions throughout the state. I do believe this began an unfettered attempt by the state officials to "plug the hole" in the dike if you will. Some ran around as if they knew nothing of the clusterfuck in the system and others ran around with a torch asking for support to revamp the prison system policies. Either way, this was concrete evidence that the state officials at best were fools. If they knew even a portion of the wrongdoings they were immoral, and if they didn't know of the wrongdoings they were inept. How did he manage to get the tits anyway? "Get your hormone shots here, before they're all gone!" "First come first served!" Well enough about Speck...point made.

I recall one pedophile, speaking of pigs, who decided that he was going to exist in population even after he was warned that this wasn't a very safe idea and even though he was in the joint for child molestation. Being a child predator was without a doubt "the cardinal sin" as far as inmates are concerned. Well this guy, needless to say, has the life expectancy of a housefly and just a blink after he hits population the guards find him with his throat slit and his own penis inserted into his mouth. Appropriate demise I believe for such an upstanding and honorable member of society. Damn, if I didn't find that humorous.

One myth I did find a little disheartening was about an inmate that had completely vanished, which added to the already ominous feeling one felt when walking the grounds of Stateville. The story went that inmates killed him many years before I had arrived on the scene and the meat from the body was used for stew. No one ever heard from this guy again. Well of course this was a myth as far as I was concerned, and just another of the many tales of terror one heard while employed as a guard. In April of 1995 while doing some construction work, a skull and some bones were found buried on the institutional grounds. These of course, were the remains of the missing convict. I guess some people unknowingly did have an interesting meal after all!

One farce stuck out in my mind, actually more than any other. I was the dreaded yearly audit. When I first started and I heard about this audit, I was scared to death. I remember thinking, "man I better be sharp and on the job today". What I noticed right off the bat was the majority of the auditors were from the employee ranks at the prison. This seemed to be at least a conflict of interest. It also seemed weird that year after year we always seemed to pass with flying colors.

Now, considering the way the prison was run on a daily basis, I found it really confusing that we did so well on an analysis that was supposed to have determined all aspects and conditions of the penitentiary. There is also a metal sign that hangs above the door to the administration building that states more or less that the American Correctional Association of America has accredited Stateville. Every time I thought about that sign a sickening feeling came over me. Either the people conducting the accreditation were literally blind or their standards were really easy to meet! Either way, just another bit of smoke and mirrors on the part of the state prison system.

Going way back to when I was discussing the art of structured termination and the like, I recall an officer that came to B-East as a new officer. He had been at the prison for a few months already but was new to our unit. He had acquired an unsavory reputation that seemed to follow him wherever he went. It was real simple, but real sad at the same time. You see, this officer was very soft spoken, and timid to put it mildly. He pretty much without fail showed up each and every day with a King James Version of the Holy Bible. Many of the officers were put off by his actions because they felt this wasn't the place for such a non-violent type of individual. Or their contention was he shouldn't flaunt his beliefs this much anyway. I on the other hand, was very put off by the other officers and their involuntary dislike of this officer.

I rather enjoyed his company, and I felt he would do his job no matter his beliefs. The rumor mill had it, that he would not shoot if on the catwalk and an officer was in trouble because he didn't believe in killing someone. Well, the good news is that theory was never tested. The bad news in my opinion is that he eventually he was fired for excessive absences or whatever.

I realize if you don't come to work you shouldn't stay employed, that goes without saying. The problem here was that no one really liked the guy, and I know for a fact that he was targeted for the structured termination technique that I mentioned earlier. This guy was getting write-ups left and right for many things that other officers could easily walk away from.

He was also mixing his beliefs with the work environment and had been warned many times to refrain from talking with inmates about religious matters and such. I do agree this is not professional per say, but then again, in what other environment would you think the word of god would be more appropriate, then in a maximum security prison were hope is not a large commodity.

My opinion on this particular subject really doesn't matter though. The only point I am trying to make here is the rules weren't the same for everyone and because of this man's good nature he was targeted. He did screw up on many occasions, but mixing those legitimate mistakes with the fabricated ones made it quite simple to eventually terminate the guy. I also understand his job is security and they have ministers at the prison for religious matters. I still think those that assisted in the firing of this guy were real close to a lawsuit. The guy never did file one as far as I know, but boy I was sure thinking of bringing my own bible and picking up were he had left off. I just plain didn't like the way the whole thing played out. This was close to the end of my time at Stateville and I had seen enough as it was, so my thinking at this point wasn't as clear as it should have been.

Let me hit a lighter note for a moment, and tell you some of my favorite stories involving some of the inmates I encountered. There was this one guy that had been in and out of prison most of his life. From the time he was old enough to get involved with gangs to the present. He had been a resident of the juvenile system many times and now had graduated to the adult end of the justice system with multiple counts of armed robbery. He had the dysfunctional family background and pretty much fit the criteria of an individual that was destined to do serious time.

The weird thing here was that this guy only robbed Kentucky Fried Chicken fast food restaurants. This fact alone humored me beyond belief, but when I found out he shot himself in the mouth while attempting suicide I was really freaked out. He apparently didn't want to go to prison, so when the police caught up with him he made the half ass attempt at ending his life. His luck as you can probably tell was usually on the bad side and he proved it here, because he just put the gun in his mouth and fired. The result was a hole that went through the back of his neck. Causing intense pain but far from the ending he was looking for. He of course wound up spending some time in the hospital prior to his court and eventual incarceration.

Some of the stories that were told to me were so blatantly stupid, that I had a hard time believing some of them. Heck, some of the inmates even got a kick out of re-telling the ignorant events that led up to their convictions. I suppose some of the stories I was told were bullshit to begin with but they were interesting anyway.

One guy was going around pretending he was a police officer using one of those little plastic badges that you can find at your local toy store. He would facilitate his sexual attacks by brandishing this little badge and quickly putting it away. When he had the attention of the victim, he would explain he needed to speak with her in private and then he would do his thing. After a few unbelievable successful ventures, if that's what you want to call them, he happens to run into a female police officer out taking her daily run. He flips out his badge and quickly replaces it in his coat, like he had successfully done so many times before, and the police officer immediately wrestles this clown to the ground and calls for back up on her cell phone.

One last story, and we'll get back to the more serious subjects. I met this inmate after I had been in B-East about a month. Of course many inmates were always trying to converse with me in an attempt to see exactly what I was all about, or if they could get over on me in one way or another. So when this inmate told me this story I thought he was pulling my chain, until he brought out the transcripts from the courtroom. He had been in the joint like six years already and was supposedly trying to get paroled, but the way I saw it, the minute the parole board reviewed the case, he more then likely would be denied on stupidity alone.

This nimrod had just robbed a gas station at gunpoint. He apparently went into the gas station and had the attendant fill up a bag with all the cash, several cartons of cigarettes, and the clerk's wallet. The alarm for the robbery had previously been set off when the clerk pulled certain bills from the register. Not to mention the fact that the clerk had wasted some of the robbers precious seconds talking to this guy, trying to convince him this robbery wasn't a wise thing to do.

The less then intelligent thief gets in his car about the exact same time that the local police are rounding the corner, and he attempts to drive away. The police immediately start their pursuit, and the thief's car dies about hundred or so yards from the gas station. You probably guessed, but this idiot was out of gas. When he told the story he was almost proud of the complete idiot he must have looked like, and he even told the story with a sly grin on his face. I was laughing so hard I almost choked.

One thing about Stateville, everything about it was implausible. From the stories that were told to me, to the events I experienced first hand. I started to build a wall like my old buddy Alec, in an attempt to keep all the dreadful or insanely mind-boggling stimuli at bay. I would tell new officers, and new residents for that matter, that they had better prepare mentally for the continual onslaught of far-fetched stimuli. Sometimes I caught my self doing a double take or asking an inmate to repeat himself because I literally couldn't believe the things I was seeing or hearing.

The thing about the population was that it was as varied as you could imagine. We had every color, nationality and personality type that you could think of. I had this one guy come into the unit and he was brand spanking new. I mean he looked like he wasn't a day over seventeen. We did of course have some really young offenders, but that too is another story. Well, he is like really fresh meat and I put him in the bullpen* until I can find him a cell assignment. The other inmates are passing by in small groups trying to get some type of first impression about the new guy and all the time this new inmate is trying to pretend that this extremely intimidating atmosphere isn't bothering him whatsoever.

He was trying so hard he really looked ridiculous. It was either that he was certifiably nuts or he had some kind of death wish, because he kept staring down inmates that could easily disassemble him and reassemble him into a cell house whore or whatever else they wanted to create with him. I waited till the inmates had dispersed for a minute and I asked him if he was affiliated. He says "Fuck No I'm not" I say, "would you like protective custody? These inmates will probably eat you alive dude." He says nothing and just rolls his eyes and sits there. So I decide I am going to let him sweat for a bit, and let the inmates pick at him a while with their verbal challenges and seasoned inmate banter.

About fifteen minutes later I finally open up the bullpen and in a firm forceful voice instruct him to pick up his box of belongings and follow me up to six gallery so we could find him a cell to stay in. As we walked up to six gallery I explained that he had to go to six because he was unassigned at the moment. I would also let him pick his new home, and that there were probably a half dozen to choose from. I had a gut feeling once he had a good look at some of the cells he would change his mind on the protective custody deal. We walked about half way down the gallery and he starts to turn around. I tell him to stop and I ask, "What the problem is?" he replies that "he decided it might be best if he goes to another unit".

Six gallery was loaded at the time with a variety of new gang-bangers right off the street. This kid that had come in on the new, looked like he was from some prestigious college or something and I knew these inmates would surely have a field day the minute he was out of my sight. I was really glad he had changed his mind.

The one thing that amazed me as well, was the diverse personality traits of the different inmates. I actually did get along with many inmates that as I reflect now, were at best cold-blooded merciless killers. One felon was doing like three life terms and another was doing like four hundred years or some such crazy sentence. Some were very intellectual and conveyed themselves in a rather academic and gentlemanly like manner at all times. I realize this might have something to do with schizophrenia or some similar malady, bit it still freaked me out just the same.

What really annoys me though, was that I felt more at ease with these society rejects then I did with some of the superiors I was supposed to be working under. At least with the inmates I had the continual presumption of impropriety on their part, and I conveyed myself with that in mind. With the different management though, I had to determine friend from foe.

I do have some memories that could be categorized in the high-quality column and with a positive theme as well.

Probably the paramount memory of all was when I was at home watching the news around super time. I had a couple days off work, and on this particular occasion I don't think I was even thinking about the prison, believe it or not! I look up from the kitchen table and the media is covering a story about an inmate at Stateville (they covered stories about Stateville all the time, just not usually positive ones) and this inmate whom I had known for a few years was being released because his conviction had been overturned.

Well this story was good in a couple of ways. First, I had gotten to know this inmate rather well and I had observed him as a model inmate to say the least. He was assigned two gallery and because of this location, I would see him several times a shift. He was a law Library clerk and plain and simple did his job and went back to his cell. He never gave me a lick of heartache, and when not at work, seemed to be always doing research on his court case. He would always tell me that he was innocent (not that all the convicts didn't say this)and he went on to say "that eventually he would be exonerated." It was nice to see that all his hard work had come to a fruitful ending! I of course believed him a bit more then the other convicts with their claims to innocence, partially because of his intelligence and less then predatory manner.

The second reason I liked the outcome of this story was not only the "good story coming from the hell hole angle", but because I really felt this man could do much more in society then incarcerated. I remember him well in the cell house and I mull over our relationship when he was confined. He was actually part of the reason I started to see the genuine changes that my persona was actually going through.

Nearing the end of my assignment in B-East, I recall our having a light argument. He was mad at the fact that over time I seemed to have fallen into the same old trap as many other officers. The continued negativity of the environment coupled with the fact of low morale amongst the officers would sometimes cause the staff to become detached and as such appearing like robots. He also felt I was starting to do everything concerning my assignment in a robotic like way, and starting to do everything that I had before proclaimed to have despised about the system.

I hate to admit it, but he was probably correct on all accusations. I was in fact completing my job in a robot like fashion and I had lost a touch of humanity to a certain extent. The kicker was I was starting to complete my duties with the presumed application that things would never change. This he felt had eroded whatever relationship we once had. He then began to look at me just like all the other mindless drones. He was right of course, my personality had taken a complete u-turn, and finally at that point, even I was beginning to see the difference.

This was another sign that my tenure at Stateville would end eventually. Looking back, I prefer to remember him walking from the front door of the prison on the nightly news. Wherever he is I wish him well. I assume by now he is a lawyer, since this seemed to be his forte and in my opinion would be the vocation that suited him best.

The Department of Corrections and the State of Illinois have made some strides in regards to their past mistakes. The completion of the Super-Max at Tamms was a start in the right direction. The redesigning of B-House into four units instead of two was also a wise move. The new designation of Pontiac Correctional Center as a Segregation style prison was another good move.

If you're going to have some control over the inmates state wide, you have to have options available to you to deal with daily insurrections and inmate belligerence. As it was, during the late eighties to the mid nineties, the hands of the state were tied in respect to repercussions that they could delve out. The inmates of course, knowing the system as they do, played on this inadequacy with a vengeance. I can only speak of the time between 1988 and 1996, but it wouldn't be presumptuous to surmise that the problems hadn't started the minute I walked into the door of the penitentiary.

They do need to make some needed changes in the way categorization of the inmates is prepared at the outset of incarceration, all the way through to the potential release. When you have inmates in the maximum-security prisons doing less then five years and other inmates in the mediums or even the minimums serving longer sentences, something needs to be done. Obviously this is a problem that needs to be addressed by several entities. The Department of Corrections houses the inmates and the courts levy the sentences. The State is in charge of overseeing the entire process.

So how do they go about these changes that are monumental at best? I have seriously contemplated an "all point" system for a long time. I do not have a degree in criminal science, correctional management, political science or any other related areas per say.

What I do have is, eight years of observing the unsuccessful cyclical methods already in use. I am also not a mathematician and as such could have some calculations a bit askew, but I will just relay the key factors of the proposal and leave the fine-tuning to those with the degrees.

The following theories are hypothetical of course and no claim is made as to the effectiveness of these theories.

Inmates are given points for abuses of the system and likewise points are subtracted for cooperation of said system.

For example...an inmate is sentenced for ten years for whatever crime. That inmate is given an established amount of points at the onset of his incarceration. Let's say, the total of those points being five points per day times the amount of days he is sentenced. IE: 5x3650 or 18250. During the screening and orientation process the inmate is advised of the point system. The point system works in a plus minus atmosphere. Lets say his mandatory prison time is 70% of his sentenced time (With good behavior of course). 70% of 18250 calculates out to 12775 points. So if this inmate doesn't do anything in abuse of the system, and likewise doesn't do anything to better himself while behind bars or participate in any work programs he would be required to spend 2555 days or 7 years behind bars. @5 points per day.

On the other hand, if lets say, he acquires a four-year degree while incarcerated; he might be eligible for a given amount of points for completion (Say 1825 points or the equivalent to one year real time). The same would go for a two-year degree (913 points or the equivalent to six months real time) or a certificate (457 points or the equivalent to 3 months real time) or simply completed classes. If for example he were involved with assignments around the prison such as painting or cooking, additional points would be subtracted from his initial allotment on a per day basis (Say 1 or 2 points per day depending on the need of said assignment).

Violation reports and the like would obviously add points to the total. A table would be worked out for violations and the spread of points the ticket committee could work with on an individual violation and per person basis. Obviously the spread of points available would be in direct relation to the amount of reports the inmate had received on any one particular violation. An inmate that had received a report for the first time would be subject to one table of points added and another inmate with two or three reports of the same violation would be subject to higher penalty points based on another table.

An example here would be the following: An inmate gets a ticket for a curtain*...he goes to the committee that's hears the ticket and if found guilty they have the option of giving 150 points (month in real time) to 450 points (three months in real time) alone or in conjunction with other penalties like commissary denial. If this inmate returns with another ticket say in a three-month period the committee might have the option of 300 to 600 points for the same violation.

The point system would be another tool, and it would be put in black and white for all to understand. Activities allowing an inmate to reduce his point total would be the different work assignments, school, church, clubs or just sitting on his ass and doing his time. An inmate could substantially reduce his time behind bars if he attains a degree, works every day and does his time in a "model inmate" way.

At first glance this system might seem a bit too complicated and bog the system down more then help it. The fact that we are in the age of instantaneous information should refute this ideology. One or two people would be responsible for putting information into the main database immediately upon any violation committee findings. At the end of each week or month, they would be also responsible for putting in the appropriate credits due the said inmate workers or the inmate simply doing his time, so that pretty much at any given time a total could be accessed for any inmate.

Lets talk about some facts and figures for a moment. Construction of Stateville Correctional Center began in 1916 and was officially opened in 1925. It originally had four round houses known as a panopticon. Currently there is only one left at Stateville and reportedly the only one left in the United States. As said previously, B-House is the longest rectangular cell house in the world spanning six hundred feet. Thirty-three foot concrete walls encompass sixty-four acres of the interior compound, along with well over two thousand acres that are adjacent to the facility. Originally built to hold a little over fifteen hundred residents, it routinely holds well over two thousand.

Almost certainly the one thing I will take with me for the rest of my days, is the sense of change I felt at "day one" compared to the feelings and thoughts I have now. I know I am different in too many ways to count at this point, in comparison to that officer fresh out of the training school.

I believe I saw an accelerated example of the change a person goes through during that long summer lockdown I told you about previously. The strange thing was I observed this metamorphosis with an inmate as the subject. That lockdown had lasted the length of one summer and I observed an inmate go from a model inmate with virtually no marks on his record at day one of the lock down, to more or less a raving lunatic by the time we let him out. This inmate would talk to me all the time during normal operations of the prison about a wide variety of things.

We became as good of friends as I would allow myself and convict to become. He was intelligent and had a good sense of humor.

Well, we lock him up on day one of the lockdown and he is as normal as ever. I would say hello in passing or whatever when I was counting or feeding and he would reply of course with some standard retort and that would be that. As each day leisurely passed by, I noticed a gradual change to those standard retorts. At first nothing you could put your finger on, but gradually he was getting a bit on the short side when responding to my daily inquiries. I did make out a report regarding the serious nature of his personality changes, if only to cover my self. I am relatively sure I observed him out of his cell once or twice and I assumed he was talking with a doctor or on a visit, and either way those seemed like good things. At least he was getting out of the cell a bit, because I could see he was loosing his grip.

We had talked about this guy in the sergeant's office a couple times and I know it was put in the sergeant's logbook. Well, by the last couple weeks of the lockdown this guy wasn't even talking to me or any other officers for that matter. He was eating and sleeping and taking care of personal hygiene but not talking whatsoever. It was as if he felt the staff was a part of the whole negative element that had him locked up in the first place. So I choose not even to attempt conversation with this inmate, with the assumption I would just feed the fire. It seemed as though he resented us as a group and he treated us individually as though we were personally responsible for leaving him in that hot cramped cell.

At this point I was starting to get concerned about many of the inmates, as more and more seemed to have negative personality changes to varied degrees. Well, we finally came off lockdown, and I am entering the unit when I hear that this particular inmate had attacked an officer the minute the officer opened his cell door. The institution had returned to normal procedures earlier during the 7-3 shift.

What I am trying to convey and how this fits as an analogy with my eight years, is this... I too started pretty jovial and in control as well. What he showed me is how a person can go from what society considers as ordinary to a all out ignoramus that has at least to some degree lost his faculties and self control. I look at his situation and all though I wasn't locked down in a very hot cell with another individual in a very disgusting cell house for an entire summer, I do see similarities to our situations. His changes were just a bit on the accelerated side in reference to the duration of time it took for those changes to actively take place.

I too went through very similar changes between day one and resignation. When I started I was as excited and optimistic as they come. He too was as cordial as you could be at day one of a presumed long lockdown. By the middle of my tenure there were distinct changes in my complete persona. He too had this problem about half way through the lockdown. By the end of the lockdown he had completely stopped functioning properly and as such was lashing out at a perceived enemy. The lengthy, lockdown had transformed him into something he wouldn't have thought he could be only months before.

My personality had also gone through decisive changes that would cause me to lash out at the assumed enemy on my last night at Stateville.

On this last night, and for the last six months or so, I was contemplating my resignation for so many reasons I couldn't even logically argue the point with myself. The only difference was on this particular shift I had been assigned to H-House and given Three-West control center as my assignment for the night. Although I was in deep thought about the future, I at least felt I had a break from the nightly circus like atmosphere. I had seen so much and been through so much, my nerves could hardly take the nightly grind. My nerves were extremely frazzled to put it mildly.

About three hours into the shift a female officer comes to my control center and says she is been ordered to relieve me. At this point, that was with out a doubt the most disparaging thing anyone could have said to me. Heading down to the sergeant's office to find out why I was being relieved and wondering were I was going, was increasingly pissing me off.

The sergeant say's "your going to B-West to feed". Well at this point I felt like that inmate behind the cell door for those three long months. With every fiber of my being I try and remain calm, while asking why I had to go to B-West rather then the female officer that relieved me.

Not to mention the fact the officer was junior to me. He explains to me, the captain said, "B-West already had a female and that he should send a male officer." I didn't have time to inquire as to why me, when there were so many male junior officers he could choose from, when what appeared to be an altered self, started screaming profanities.

I was doing all I could to restrain the totally out of control dual personality when I decided just go to B-West and tuff it out. When I arrived at B-West I was assigned the galleries of course and I decided this was the last time I would walk the galleries.

I had a little while before we would begin to feed so I decided that I would go to the captain's office and type a short but sweet resignation. I did do just that and the following morning I walked up to personnel and handed them the note along with my badge and identification. It wasn't this one event that caused my continual decline as an officer. It took eight years of events such as these for Stateville to finally claim victory.

I walked from the institution to my car for the last time with an enormous sense of relief. As I drove home reality started to come back to me. Enough anyway, that I realized I had just given up, and everyone had told me that eventually I would do just that. Sure it had taken eight years for the Stateville blender to have its way. Nonetheless I still had succumbed, and had in fact given up. I too, like the inmate had lost all my mental faculties in such a way as too totally reverse my life and send myself free falling into a depressive precipice. For at least the next two years I would fight trying to attain some degree of mental balance.

If I had just one thing to say as a last thought, it would have to be this: "The inmates and the staff are not corporate cannon-fodder!" They are real people with real emotions. When the state or administrations make decisions, they need to be sure it's in the best interest of all those that the decisions effect. It's not always about the all mighty dollar. The administrations of the future need to be concerned about the individual institution and not how Springfield is going to react to unforeseen events or needed changes. Though the administration and the state would like you to believe that everything that occurs is not related:

THE GENERAL PUBLIC ARE THE FINAL SOUNDING BOARD, AND THEY ALONE SHOULD BE THE ONES TO DECIDE IF THE EVENTS THAT TRANSPIRE ON A DAILY BASIS BEHIND THE WALLS ARE INFACT ... "ISOLATED INCIDENTS!"

*Kevin L. Thomas*

# Glossary

1. Brick- One carton of cigarettes sometimes used as currency.
2. Brothers- designation of fellow gang members or sometimes allied gang members.
3. Bullpen- A temporary holding cell used for incoming or outgoing inmates.
4. Catwalk- Walkway used by armed officers to protect officers on the galleries.
5. Cellie- Nickname given to the person you are housed with.
6. Circle- Immediate area around Dining Room Tower used for feeding the inmates.
7. CS Gas- Canister filled with powder based gas used for inmate control.
8. C.O.Ts- Uncomplimentary designation for Correctional Officer Trainees.
9. Curtain- Item used to block view to the inside of cells, usually a bed sheet.
10. DRT- Dining Room Tower.
11. F-House -Round or Panopticon cell house primarily used for most aggressive inmates.
12. Flag- Lower most gallery and foundation of cell house.
13. GDs- Gangster Disciples; Chicago area largest gang. Colors: Blue and Black.
14. Greenshirt- Correctional officers.
15. H-House- Unit used for protective custody inmates. Referred to as "Punk City".
16. Hooch- Homemade wine usually made from a variety of juices, sugar and fresh fruit.
17. Industry- The buildings that house the Furniture Factory, Soap Shop and Taylor Shop.
18. Juice- Assumed prison influence usually associated with high echelon gang members.

19. Kites- Prison letters or notes passed from one inmate to another.
20. K3 Units- Whiteshirts such as Captains, Lieutenants or above.
21. LDs- Latin Disciples; Allied with Gangsters Disciples; Colors: Blue and Black.
22. LKs- Latin Kings; Allied with Vice Lords; Colors: Yellow and Black.
23. Lines- Group of inmates going from one place to another.
24. Lockdown- Status of Institution after a major disturbance. All inmates secure.
25. MCs- Mickey Cobras; allied with Vice Lords; Colors: Red and Black.
26. Neutron- Independent inmate although usually connected to one of the gangs.
27. Population- Inmates in customary prison environment with standard privileges.
28. Sanction- The pact between gangs for consistency on a given act or agreement.
29. Shakedown- Search for contraband on an inmates person, cell or belongings.
30. Shank- Homemade knife made from random items found throughout inside the prison.
31. State and Madison- Walkway linking a variety of structures on prison grounds.
32. Unassigned- Inmates just entering the institution or not assigned to job in the prison.
33. Umbrella- Term referring to an inmate not actually in a gang, but affiliated.
34. Unit G- Unit usually reserved for inmates assigned to the industry department.
35. Unit I- Unit used primarily for disciplinary or administrative segregation purposes.
36. Unit X- Unit housing protective custody overflow or administrative protective custody.

37. Vice Lords- Allied with MCs and LKs; Colors: Red and Black.
38. Violation- Assault on an inmate by another, varying from simple to sexual assault.
39. Whiteshirt- Major, Captains or Lieutenants.
40. Writs- The taking of an inmate from the prison to an outside activity such as court.
41. 434- Incident report used to advise the administration of abnormal occurrences.
42. 10-10- A fight or other major insurrection.
43. ADs- Administrative Directives.
44. DRs- Departmental Regulations.

# About the Author

Author Kevin L. Thomas is forty-two years of age, has three children, and has been married twenty-three years. He is currently writing his second novel, *The Purple Elephant*, a fictional thriller. Jack-of-all-trades, master of few, Kevin is aspiring to be a famous writer of many genres, keeping his works controversial and thought-provoking.